Welfare Realities

Welfare Realities

From Rhetoric to Reform

MARY JO BANE
DAVID T. ELLWOOD

Harvard University Press

Cambridge, Massachusetts
London, England

Library of Congress Cataloging-in-Publication Data

Bane, Mary Jo.
Welfare realities : from rhetoric to reform / Mary Jo Bane, David
T. Ellwood.
    p. cm.
Includes bibliographical references (p. 201) and index.
ISBN 0-674-94912-9 (cloth)
ISBN 0-674-94913-7 (pbk.)
1. Aid to families with dependent children programs—United States. 2. Public
welfare—United States. I. Ellwood, David T. II. Title.
HV699.B36 1994
362.5'82'0973—dc20   93-45029
                                                                              CIP

To Ken and Marilyn

Contents

Preface

When the topic of welfare comes up, the dialogue often turns angry and judgmental; the prose becomes purple. All sides draw stark images and speak in tones of moral outrage. Debates turn ugly. And just below the surface, indeed sometimes well above the surface, are often vicious racial stereotypes. There is much heat and very little light.

This book was written in the belief that facts, ideas, and ideals can cut through at least some of the rhetoric and point to thoughtful policy. The chapters represent nearly a decade of our work on the reality of welfare. We have pulled together, revised, updated, and sometimes reversed the findings of a series of papers we have written over the years that have been widely circulated, but never fully published. They have languished as reports and photocopies in classrooms and congressional offices alike.

The chapters cover a broad landscape, ranging from the nature of welfare offices to the duration and dynamics of welfare to explanations for welfare "dependency" to policy proposals, both modest and bold. Each chapter attempts what is nearly impossible: to examine welfare, its recipients, its providers, and the swirl of policy ideas with calm and clarity.

Even for two people with strong academic backgrounds, individual values and personal experiences must color the analysis. Our perspectives have especially been shaped by the institutions in which we have done our work. All of Ellwood's and most of Bane's research was done while each was professor of public policy at Harvard University's Kennedy School of Government. Bane's chapters also reflect her experience as Executive Deputy Commissioner and later Commissioner of the New York State Department of Social Services. Thomas J. Kane, first author of Chapter 1, is assistant professor of public policy at the Kennedy School.

As we complete this preface, we have both joined a new administration in Washington, D.C. We face perhaps the toughest challenge of all: to help steer a process of welfare reform in an intensely political environment. Bane serves as Assistant Secretary for Children and Families in the Department of Health and Human Services and oversees many of the federal welfare and children's programs. Ellwood is Assistant Secretary for Planning and Evaluation in the same department, overseeing major policy development and evaluation work there.

It is essential to note that the research for this book was complete before we took our government positions. The chapters represent our findings and positions before we began our current jobs. We are already encountering new realities, both empirical and political, that will affect some of our descriptions and prescriptions. As always, our views of this complex set of issues are open to change. We believe that most of the research here will stand the test of time.

What Is Welfare?

Conversation and legislation about welfare and welfare reform usually focus on the program known as Aid to Families with Dependent Children (AFDC). In 1992 the AFDC program provided cash assistance to about 4.7 million families per month at a cost to the federal government of about $13 billion (U.S. House 1993, pp. 679, 685).

The AFDC program accounts for only 1 percent of total federal spending, but it receives a much greater share of public attention. In part this attention stems from common perceptions of who AFDC recipients are, some of which are accurate and others of which are highly stereotyped. Most AFDC recipients are single mothers with children. The typical welfare family in the early 1990s was made up of a never-married mother in her twenties or thirties with one or two children. The marital status of AFDC recipients changed importantly over the 1970s and 1980s. In 1973 the typical recipient was divorced or separated from the father of her children. By 1990, 54 percent of the children on AFDC had mothers who had never been married to their father.

In 1990 about 40 percent of welfare recipients were non-Hispanic white, 40 percent were black, and 17 percent were Hispanic. Most lived in metropolitan areas, though typically not in inner-city ghettos. The average family size for AFDC cases was 2.9 persons, down from 3.6 in 1973. About half of all AFDC recipients lived in six large, highly urbanized states: California, New York, Illinois, Ohio, Michigan, and Pennsylvania.

Plan of the Book

Even these few demographic facts suggest the diversity of the AFDC population. This book documents many other aspects of diversity, particularly in the duration of AFDC receipt and in the prospects facing AFDC recipients. It also asks, and tries to answer, a number of other questions about welfare. How did the welfare system come to be the way we know it? Why has the culture of welfare proved so hard to change? Why do some recipients seem to be trapped in dependency? How can we reform the current system—or should we replace it?

Chapter 1, by Kane and Bane, draws on Kane's fieldwork in a welfare office in New England, where he studied client-caseworker interactions. Some parts of the chapter are reworked from Kane (1990) and other portions are based on a paper in Pechman (1992). The chapter identifies what we believe to be a major problem with welfare as we know it: an administrative culture that is more concerned with the enforcement of eligibility rules and with making sure that recipients comply with AFDC regulations than with helping clients toward self-sufficiency. The eligibility-compliance culture makes the welfare system appear both adversarial and mysterious to the clients it is supposed to serve.

The current system discourages clients from working not only through its financial incentives but also through its bureaucratic impediments. To work is to risk becoming classified as "error prone": an administrative nuisance to a welfare worker whose primary job is to make sure that no client receives more welfare benefits than she is due. Reformers—particularly the authors of the Family Support Act of 1988—have taken steps to build into the welfare system a different set of expectations, in which it is understood that the primary task of welfare is to help clients attain self-sufficiency. This process is proving to be a difficult one, however, because the eligibility-compliance culture is now deeply rooted.

Chapter 2 consolidates and updates a decade of quantitative research originally reported in three unpublished papers: Bane and Ellwood (1983) and Ellwood (1986a,b). This research documented a view of welfare receipt as a dynamic process involving a diverse mix of mothers with different needs. One of our earliest findings was that most people who begin to receive welfare do so for a relatively brief spell, but that the average spell length for those receiving welfare at any point in time is much longer, because people with long spells pile up on the caseload. This finding suggested the need to examine more closely the dynamics of welfare use by different groups.

The chapter also documents our evolving views about welfare dynamics. As our research progressed, we began to pay more attention to the total time women spend on welfare, combining both first and repeat spells. This concept led to our conclusion that welfare receipt was even more of a long-term proposition than we had originally thought. We also began to focus more on the "cycling" dynamic—going on and off of welfare repeatedly—which has now been well documented by LaDonna Pavetti (1993).

Understanding *why* some people receive welfare for a long time is Ellwood's focus in Chapter 3. This chapter identifies three models that have been used to explain "dependency." Choice theory emphasizes the choices made by recipients and the structure of incentives that they face. Expectancy theory emphasizes the way that social and economic institutions shape recipients' self-confidence and sense of control of their fate. Class-cultural theories emphasize the values and culture that often exist in centers of concentrated urban poverty.

The theories are tested against the accumulating body of evidence regarding welfare use, poverty, and dependency. We find that rational choice theory, supplemented with expectancy theory, explains welfare dynamics reasonably well, but with some significant limitations. Widely divergent results can result from modest changes in assumptions. Rational choice theory cannot explain many of the changes in family structure, welfare use, and poverty that have been occurring over the past several decades. Persistent inner-city poverty is a particularly difficult conundrum that no theory explains very well. We conclude that no theory offers a definitive explanation of dependency or suggests policy prescriptions likely to offer a quick fix to problems of long-term dependency.

In the final two chapters (written well before we joined the U.S. Department of Health and Human Services and neither meant to reflect administration policy), we offer suggestions for changing the welfare system. Chapters 4 and 5 offer two different perspectives on reform, which we see as counterpoints to each other. They reflect our somewhat different perspectives as program operator and policy analyst.

In Chapter 4, Bane draws on her experiences as a program manager in New York, where she became convinced of the importance of understanding program operations at the street level. Her participation in the design and operation of a small modified version of child support insurance represented our first real attempt to put our ideas into practice.

Chapter 4 offers several prescriptions for a welfare system that encourages self-sufficiency. It stresses the continued importance of the transitional educational, employment, and training services envisioned by the authors of the JOBS program. But these programs must not fall into the trap of the eligibility-compliance culture of the older WIN program. Employment programs must be designed and implemented with a commitment to clear expectations that program recipients work or prepare for work. More control and encouragement should be given to those who do work. Chapter 4 also argues that we should return rationality and fairness to the benefit structure, to make welfare more comprehensible and legitimate to those who use it and to those who pay for it. This chapter draws on Bane and Dowling (1985) and Bane (1989).

In Chapter 5, Ellwood lays out ideas for reducing poverty by replacing welfare. He suggests that government aid should be designed to encourage work and family responsibility. Work should be made to pay, so that those who work are not poor. As the research reviewed in Chapter 3 indicates, welfare as we know it is structured so that those who work are no better off than if they had remained on welfare. Through wage and tax policy and health care for the working poor, work must be made to be the right choice for those whose other choice is welfare. The policy suggestions in Chapter 5 also reflect a conviction that one parent should not be expected to do the work of two. Single parents should not be expected both to provide child care and to be full-time breadwinners. The chapter explores the need for a new system of child support enforcement and insurance that combines tough enforcement with a guaranteed benefit. If work can be made to pay, and if both parents can be made to support their children, we may be able to reform welfare so that it is a transitional, time-limited program to assist those who face periods of unusual need. Welfare as we know it may prove to be something we can do without.

In a decade of work, we have been aided by so many people that we cannot possibly do them justice. We have learned from the comments of so many researchers in the field that we hesitate to list them for fear of leaving someone off the list. Nevertheless, we cite a few who have deeply influenced the research and ideas presented here. The thoughts and support of Henry Aaron, Robert Behn, Rebecca Blank, Sheldon Danziger, Michael Dowling, Tim Downe, Greg Duncan, Irwin Garfinkel, Robert Greenstein, Judy Gueron, Christopher Jencks, Thomas Kane, Robert Lerman, Frank Levy, Michael Lipsky, Rebecca Maynard, Daniel Patrick Moynihan, Wendell Primus, Lee Rainwater, Lawrence Summers, Michael Wiseman, Julie Wilson, and William Julius Wilson stand out in particular. Our debt is even greater to the graduate students and research assistants who labored long hours to produce many of the quantitative results in this book, who shaped our ideas and interpretations of what we saw, and who compiled this work for the book.

LaDonna Pavetti deserves particular mention, for without her this book would never have been completed. She spent hours supervising, programming, editing, and checking our updates and revisions. She pointed out flaws in our logic and places where more recent data seemed at odds with our earlier conclusions. And she nudged, even goaded us into finally completing the book. Naomi Goldstein also deserves high praise, for she too was essential both to the original research and to pulling together this work. She too worked tirelessly to help us finish the project. Best of all, on top of their many intellectual and managerial talents, these colleagues are warm and wonderful people.

We also want to thank Karl Eschbach for his fine editing and analysis. Marian Valliant did much of the empirical work in this updated version, along with Gina Raimondo. Their careful work and unfailing good humor are greatly appreciated.

The papers that served as the foundation for the chapters were produced in large part through the efforts of John Dacey and Erica Groshen. Their work with the Panel Study of Income Dynamics and their help in preparing earlier papers have been essential.

Through the years, our research on welfare has been funded chiefly from three sources: the Ford Foundation, the Russell Sage Foundation, and the Department of Health and Human Services. We will always feel indebted to Robert Curvin, Pru Brown, Gordon Berlin, Alice O'Connor, John Lanigan, Eric Wanner, and Dan Weinberg among many others for their generous intellectual and financial help. They provided support at a time when research on welfare was not particularly fashionable, and long before we had any real track record. Some of the work here was also done under grants or contracts provided to Mathematica Policy Research, Urban Systems Research and Engineering, and Brandeis University, to whom we served as consultants. These organizations were extremely helpful as well.

We were also supported by the Malcolm Wiener Center for Social Policy at the John F. Kennedy School of Government at Harvard University. The generosity of Malcolm Wiener and his extraordinary intellectual breadth have been inspiring. The people at the Center are wonderful. Where else can one find so many brilliant and compassionate individuals? We are particularly grateful to Frank Hartmann, Joan Curhan, Shelly Coulter, and especially Julie Wilson for everything they have done.

Naturally, none of these people or institutions bears any responsibility for flaws in this work. The policy views expressed here are only those of the authors. And we emphasize that these in no way represent the views of President Clinton or his administration.

Most important are our families. David's children, Malinda and Andrea, have given so very much to their father. This book is dedicated to our spouses, Ken and Marilyn. They have played a crucial role in our thinking and our values from the start. Their love and affection coupled with their powerful moral and intellectual integrity are central to everything we do.

Welfare Realities

1

The Context for Welfare Reform

In the fall of 1988, Congress passed and the President signed what was billed as the most comprehensive welfare reform bill since the passage of the Social Security Act in the 1930s. This bill, the Family Support Act (FSA), had as its purpose "to replace the existing AFDC program with a new Family Support Program which emphasizes work, child support and need-based family support supplements, . . . [and] to encourage and assist needy children and parents under the new program to obtain the education, training and employment needed to avoid long-term welfare dependency" (U.S. Congress 1988).

Passing the Family Support Act was a long and tortuous process, involving politically difficult decisions and compromises. Congress was rightfully proud of itself for taking an important step, and no doubt felt that it was finished with welfare reform for the foreseeable future.

By 1993, however, welfare reform was once again on the agenda of the President and of most governors, as though the FSA had already become an irrelevance or a failure. By encouraging states to apply for waivers from federal mandates, the Bush administration had encouraged a wave of state experimentation with incentives and requirements aimed at shaping work and family formation. Before any of these innovations or the FSA itself has been carefully evaluated or even fully implemented, the nation is likely to see a new round of welfare reform, focusing on issues of time limitation, mandatory work, and child support.

1

Recent history suggests that welfare reform is likely to be a continuing dilemma and preoccupation. In this context, it is worthwhile to examine the characteristics of the current welfare system and the history on which the newest welfare reforms build. The Family Support Act was an attempt to redirect a vast system's efforts from simply monitoring the eligibility of families on AFDC toward enabling more of those families to make the transition to self-sufficiency. Such a change is not simply a matter of changing eligibility rules. Rather, it represents a dramatic shift from an organizational culture in which the dominant ethos is centered around eligibility and compliance to one in which clients and welfare workers are engaged in the common tasks of finding work, arranging child care, and so on. The distinction is more than a matter of semantics. Whether a work requirement is understood as a route out of welfare or as just another prerequisite for continued eligibility is a subtle but crucial difference for the behavior of both clients and front-line workers.

To understand the current state of the welfare system, and thus the current context of welfare reform, we believe it is necessary to understand how the current system has come to emphasize eligibility and compliance to the exclusion of nearly every other goal.

The Client-Caseworker Relationship

The AFDC program is a federal-state partnership, with a good deal of state-to-state variation in how the program operates. There is, however, enough commonality to allow a general description of how the system works. The following is based on observations in a New England welfare office in 1988.

A mother applying for assistance, upon locating the office of the Division of Income Maintenance (DIM), stands in line to speak with the glass-encased receptionist at the front of a waiting room holding roughly seventy-five chairs arranged in rows. Although only five to ten people may be waiting in line to speak with the receptionist, many of the chairs may be filled and there may be children running about the room—especially on Mondays or Fridays, when most people rush to get their business done before or after the weekend.

Other people standing in line may be there to give additional documentation to their workers—rent receipts, wage stubs, change of address forms—to question the amount of their check, or to apply for emergency housing after being evicted. When the woman reaches the front of the line, her name is put on the bottom of the list of those waiting for screening interviews.

The list of new applications is under the direction of a supervisor of one of the "intake units," consisting of workers who specialize in initial interviews and eligibility determinations for new applicants. These workers—acknowledged by other workers as the elite line workers in the office hierarchy because they "set the tone," or establish the pattern, for later agency-client interactions—take applications on a rotating basis (Handler and Hollingsworth 1971). When they are not actually conducting interviews (which is approximately 50 percent of the time), they are collecting the verifications for earlier applications, making determinations, or doing other follow-up tasks.

When her name is called, the new applicant is led down a hallway into a much larger room filled with cubicles containing other new applicants and intake workers, or other workers speaking with ongoing claimants. To start, the intake worker asks her whether she has received welfare in the state before and asks to see her social security number. With this information, the worker turns to a computer terminal in the cubicle to verify the applicant's statement—checking whether or not she has indeed made a previous application, whether it was granted or not, and the reasons for her termination. Self-declarations are rarely accepted. The worker will verify nearly every statement related to eligibility. "Have you ever lived on Peabody Street?" the worker might ask, finding a case with a similar name in past records.

The worker then begins to try to identify the programs for which the person may be eligible. Does she have any dependent children? Is she pregnant? Is the father present? Does she or the father work? Does she or the father have any disabilities? Pulling out the relevant application forms, the worker prompts the applicant for responses as she runs through the application sequentially. The intake worker starts with household composition: who lives in the household, their

names, and how they are related to the applicant. Whether children
live with her, their age, and their number are all crucial to the
potential benefit amount, and the worker requests birth certificates
to prove at least their existence and age.

Many applicants know to bring birth certificates to their initial
interview. But the worker will list additional verifications needed on
a separate sheet of paper for the client to return later. For instance,
depending upon the programs for which she is applying, the applicant may be instructed to bring in birth certificates for the children
if she has not already done so; certification that she applied for and
was denied other benefits such as unemployment insurance or social
security disability insurance; utility bills; rent receipts or letters from
past and present landlords verifying residence (to prevent one recipient from collecting at various addresses and/or from neighbor-
ing states); copies of past and present bank account statements, from
as long as two years previous; social security cards for everyone in
the family; if anyone in the family has life insurance, a letter from
the company naming the beneficiary and the cash surrender value;
verification of school attendance from the children's schools; copies
of car registrations and titles; pay stubs; if pregnant, a letter from
the doctor stating estimated due date; marriage or divorce papers.
Depending upon the case, there may be fifteen to twenty verifications that the applicant will have to furnish before being termed
eligible. In the coming weeks, the mother will have to visit a number
of other public and private institutions, standing in line to obtain
the requisite paperwork: the Bureau of Vital Statistics for birth
certificates, the Social Security Administration for cards or proof of
application for disability insurance, possibly the Unemployment
Office, the offices of the local utilities and the Department of Motor
Vehicles.

At the end of the intake interview, which typically lasts sixty to
ninety minutes, the worker hands the applicant the list of required
verifications. Although the intake interview is over, the applicant is
not likely to be able to leave the office yet. If the woman is pregnant,
she will be directed back to the waiting room to wait to see the Early
Periodic Screening and Diagnostic Testing (EPSDT) program
worker to verify her prenatal care arrangements. Whether or not

she is currently pregnant, she will be instructed to wait to see someone from the child support unit to identify the father of her children and to pursue a support order.

Over the next few weeks, the applicant will collect all of the necessary verifications and bring them in to the receptionist. In the meantime, the department will pursue computer matches with the unemployment insurance wage database, with banks, and with other databases. (In New York City, they even cross-check the list of hot dog vendors for unreported earnings.) The department will make a determination on the applicant's eligibility within thirty days. If she does not bring in all of the needed verifications, her application will be denied.

If she is determined eligible, any recipient without children under three years of age will be required to make an appointment with the Department of Human Resources to register for a work and training program. Though the local human resources and income maintenance offices are usually located in the same building, there is virtually no contact between the two other than verification that the recipient has registered for the program.

Once a client is determined to be eligible, her eligibility must be verified at least once every six months. The first redetermination interview may be held three months after the first check is issued, when an individual is asked to verify again any aspects of her eligibility that are likely to have changed—such as any changes in household size or earnings. After this, the redeterminations are usually held every six months, although "error-prone" cases may be subject to redetermination more often. After the case has been granted, each client is assigned to a particular "eligibility technician," who will handle each aspect of that person's eligibility from that point forward. (Each eligibility technician handles approximately two hundred ongoing cases.) In addition to periodic redeterminations, clients are likely to contact their worker with questions about their check, when they move, when their household composition changes, when they are in danger of eviction, when the food stamp amount is incorrect, and when similar problems arise. If the person also works, then she will have to fill out another form and mail or deliver her pay stubs from each month.

Several characteristics of the relationship between a client and the department deserve comment. First, note that the basis for every interaction between the recipient and the worker was eligibility. From the beginning, each question the worker asked was aimed at learning for which programs the applicant might be eligible and later focused specifically on each point of eligibility. Cooperation with the child-support enforcement team was presented to the recipient as a condition of eligibility for welfare. Similarly, participation in the work and training program was offered not as a route to self-sufficiency but as a compliance requirement for staying on welfare—much like bringing in a rent receipt or a utility bill.

Second, in each exchange, the Division of Income Maintenance worker controls the pace and content of the interaction, as dictated by the eligibility forms the department provides. This serves at least two purposes. Because no room is left for any extraneous information to enter the exchange, the process protects the worker from overextension, from feeling compelled to help in other aspects of a client's life, and from being tempted to make exceptions to the rules based on extenuating circumstances. Such protection is crucial when workers are carrying caseloads of two hundred or more. Another purpose served by the nature of the interaction is that it reinforces the worker's underlying need for the client's compliance. A worker carrying a heavy caseload has very little time for any interaction between worker and client on topics other than those directly related to eligibility. An uncooperative client can prove quite troublesome. As a result, the intake worker's job is recognized within the local office as vital in setting the tone for later interactions.

Third, the requirements of establishing and maintaining eligibility demand a large portion of a client's time and problem-solving capability. Beyond the hours required to come in and stand in line at the DIM office, a client spends a considerable amount of time simply collecting the required verifications.

Fourth, the process actually discourages efforts at self-support. A woman who finds a part-time job, and thus has earnings that vary from week to week, becomes an "error-prone" case and is scheduled for redeterminations more often. For a client to find a part-time job also means more work for her ongoing worker, who is required to monitor monthly income reports.

There is little in the relationship between recipients and line workers that would aid a recipient in putting together the necessary child support, child care arrangements, training, and employment necessary to become self-supporting. Rather, by encouraging passivity, by focusing the recipient's attention solely on the problem of maintaining eligibility, by discouraging movements toward self-support, the nature of worker-client interactions may hinder clients' efforts at becoming self-sufficient.

Eligibility rules are critically important to both clients and workers. The rules rationalize the decisions of workers and circumscribe their obligations to clients who often have needs that would otherwise overwhelm those who work with them. For the clients, the eligibility rules provide legitimacy to their dependency and continued need for financial support. The behavior of clients and workers in focusing upon the eligibility rules is therefore reinforcing.

The eligibility-compliance culture that characterizes the current welfare system contrasts sharply with what we might call a self-sufficiency culture. A self-sufficiency culture would structure interactions and expectations around work and preparation for work, with most of the attention of clients and workers devoted to moving off welfare rather than to validating the credentials for staying on it. Even before the current wave of welfare reform, there have been various attempts over the years to add self-sufficiency programs to the welfare system. Often, however, these have turned out to be simply add-ons to the basic welfare system, rather than a real change in culture. When the dominant paradigm is founded upon eligibility, employment programs may be interpreted by clients and workers alike to be merely another requirement for continued receipt, just like bringing in a birth certificate or a utility bill.

To understand the two cultures, we examine the history of the welfare system from two perspectives: first, the development of the eligibility-compliance culture over a social casework model, and second, the attempts to bring self-sufficiency programs into the welfare system.

The Casework Model, 1962–1967

The early sixties saw the first attempt at widespread implementation of a casework model for the provision of social services. As the civil rights struggle and events such as the publication of Michael Harrington's *The Other America* (1962) focused the nation's attention on the problem of poverty, federal administrators were selling the new service provision model to Congress as a way to reduce poverty and cut the welfare rolls at the same time. In *The Other America*, the problems of poor people were described as being much more than simply a lack of money. According to Martha Derthick, "Services began to be presented to political leaders—and by them to the public—as a means to a widely shared goal: 'rehabilitation of the poor,' 'an end to dependency,' and 'restoration of self-support'" (Derthick 1970, p. 159). Although the notion that poverty could be combated with counseling was not novel—for instance, private philanthropists, known as "friendly visitors," had played that role decades before—public provision of such counseling services through the welfare system had never been widespread in the United States (Katz 1983, 1986).

The most important legislation leading to the new emphasis on social services came with the Social Security Amendments of 1962. The amendments raised federal compensation for administrative costs attributable to services from 50 percent to 75 percent. Among the services required to qualify for the higher matching rate was the development of a "social study" for each child on the AFDC rolls, 2.8 million in 1962. The study was to include "a description of each child and a statement as to his mental and physical condition, his school progress if applicable, any defined problems that are identified, and plans to meet such problems" (N.Y. DSW 1963). A caseworker working with families with "defined service" needs (80 to 90 percent of AFDC families) was supposed to have a maximum of sixty cases, and there were to be no more than five workers per supervisor (though few states actually met the requirement). Workers were encouraged to contact school personnel, neighbors, and relatives in evaluating home conditions and educational achievement. In an initial description of how to do a social study, the New

York Department of Social Welfare instructed workers to inspect the home environment closely:

> The worker will obtain much information about the general atmosphere of the home he visits through his ability to observe and to understand what he sees. Are relationships congenial or unfriendly? Does one member of the household hold a dominant or domineering position? Is one over-critical of the others? Are parents or guardians aware of, and interested in meeting, the needs of children? (N.Y. DSW 1963, p. 31)

As in other states, the same workers who handled a client's AFDC eligibility determinations could initiate court proceedings to remove the child from the home if this were deemed necessary.

Because of the "social study" requirement, the 1962 amendments were an important influence on how caseworkers were deployed. The primary setting for contact between worker and client, rather than being a welfare office or an interviewing booth, became the client's home. The new emphasis on "home visits" was significant in a number of respects. First, the ambiguity of the scope of workers' responsibilities resulted in high "burn-out" rates. Many workers were faced with a much wider variety of client needs—substandard housing, home violence, alcoholism, lack of child care—for which they had neither the time to respond themselves nor any program to which to refer clients (Bell 1973). Second, workers found themselves in a difficult predicament: they needed to establish an ongoing trusting relationship with clients but also to verify their eligibility carefully. Carrying heavy caseloads and hoping to avoid conflict, some workers were tempted to "look the other way" when faced with improprieties such as another adult's presence or unreported earnings (Handler and Hollingsworth 1971). As a result, 26.5 percent of all AFDC payments in New York were overpayments or payments to ineligible families as late as 1973. The national average was 16 percent in that year (SSA–OPEQ 1980). A third effect of the field deployment of workers was an increase in applications. Placing caseworkers in the neighborhoods lowered the barriers to applying.

The promoters of the amendments of 1962 had envisioned a radical change in the nature of welfare administration. In testifying before Congress, Secretary Ribicoff claimed, "We have a realistic program which will pay dividends on every dollar invested. It can move some persons off the assistance rolls entirely, enable others to attain a higher degree of self-confidence and independence, [and] encourage children to grow strong in mind and body" (Handler and Hollingsworth 1971, p. 104). President Kennedy referred to the 1962 amendments as the "most far-reaching revision of our public welfare program since it was enacted in 1935" (CIR 1980, p. 51).

Unfortunately, although the amendments resulted in the hiring of thousands of caseworkers and possibly began to relieve the punitive tone of welfare administration, very few new "hard" services were actually developed and delivered. For the most part, the "services" that were provided were largely the interactions between caseworkers and clients. There were very few programs aimed at issues such as job training, alcoholism, and parental violence to which workers could actually refer clients.

In the late 1960s Joel Handler and Ellen Jane Hollingsworth studied the daily interactions of workers and recipients in six counties in Wisconsin. They found, first, that worker home visits were infrequent (usually only once every two to three months) and brief (averaging forty minutes). Second, because of high worker turnover and the infrequency of visits, a client would see the same worker on average no more than three times, totaling roughly two hours. Even the most effective counselors would have difficulty making much headway given such short, sporadic exposures. Third, the content of their interactions rarely focused on "hard" services, special programs, or future plans for self-sufficiency.

The Handler and Hollingsworth evidence suggests a low level of actual social service activity of the kind envisioned by the framers of the 1962 amendments. Indeed, they concluded that such "social service activity is little more than a relatively infrequent, pleasant chat" (Handler and Hollingsworth 1971, pp. 126–127). According to one social work historian, "The general idea was to change from merely giving needy people more money to arranging with them a deliberate plan to make the best of their situation" (Leiby 1978, p. 304). In the end, however, very few of such services were offered. Winifred Bell summarized: "Federal administrators could hope, dream, guide and exhort, but they could not deliver" (Bell 1973, pp. 66–67).

The 1962 amendments failed to generate many "hard" services for several reasons. Rather than limit the new 75 percent reimbursement rate to "new" services, federal administrators allowed 75 percent reimbursement for virtually any costs associated with a family with "defined service need" in order to entice states to comply. What constituted an eligible service was rarely defined. Another important problem was the lack of training among the staffs of local welfare offices. There were approximately 35,000 caseworker positions nationwide in 1960 (Steiner 1966, p. 183), but fewer than 2,400 graduate students in social work each year. The human capital for providing professional casework services to the entire caseload was simply not available to the welfare system in 1962 (Derthick 1970).

Though the Social Security Amendments of 1962 had an important impact on the deployment of welfare workers, the goal of promoting self-sufficiency with a network of professional caseworkers remained elusive. The primary force generating change in this first period had come from federal administrators and from the developing social work profession; the initiative for the second phase of change was to come from outside the public welfare bureaucracy.

The Legal Rights Movement and the End of Casework, 1967–1972

Between 1962 and 1967, AFDC rolls had grown by 36 percent, an annual average growth rate of 6.3 percent (SSA 1989). The casework model was not working as promised; the caseload was increasing, not declining. By 1967 those in Congress who were calling for greater restrictions were gaining ground. In discussing a bill to impose work requirements in 1967, Chairman Wilbur Mills of the House Committee on Ways and Means held the states responsible for the continued growth in the AFDC caseload:

> We have . . . the thought in mind that it takes requirements on the states to reverse these trends. In 1962 we gave them options.

For five years this load has gone up and up and up, with no end in sight. . . . Are you satisfied with the fact that illegitimacy in this country is rising and rising and rising? I am not. . . . Now we are requiring them to do something about it. . . . [We] are not going to continue to put federal funds into states for the benefit of parents when they refuse to get out of the house and try to earn something. (ACIR 1980, p. 57)

The resulting amendments of 1967 established the Work Incentive (WIN) program requiring registration of parents except those with young children in work and training programs, mandated that the states provide child-care services to participants in those programs, and lessened the implicit tax rate on earnings by disregarding the first $30 and one third of the remainder in computing income.

The Welfare Rights Movement

Although Congress may not have been inclined to let the program grow after 1967, forces at work outside of the federal and state welfare agencies led to a great acceleration in welfare spending. The expansion during the 1960s had been largely due to initiatives from within government (primarily the federal government)—the establishment of AFDC-UP for families with two parents in 1962, the provision of Medicaid in 1965, the 1962 amendments and the proliferation of casework, and the efforts of federal administrators to lessen the "punitive" nature of welfare provision. The growth in welfare expenditures after 1967, however, was largely due to external pressures. In the original Social Security legislation, the federal government was obliged to match a given percentage of state expenditures on welfare. As long as people continued to present themselves at local offices and continued to be found eligible, the federal government was required to match state benefit payments. To take advantage of this, the new Welfare Rights Organization, led by George Wiley, organized residents of poor neighborhoods to apply for welfare (Piven and Cloward 1971).

As a result, between 1967 and 1972, the number of applications for AFDC surged dramatically and welfare rolls more than doubled, with an annual average growth of 16.9 percent per year. The hiring of public welfare personnel had outpaced the growth in the caseload between 1962 and 1967 because of federal maximum caseload standards, but after 1967, the growth in the caseload swamped the growth in personnel (SSA 1989; unpublished tabulations from the U.S. Bureau of the Census). Denial rates fell as the ability of states to process the new applications was strained (Piven and Cloward 1977).

The organization of welfare clients and the resulting orchestration of legal challenges had at least two important effects on local office administration: first, the easing of some of the administrative deterrents to applying for welfare and, second, the consolidation of grants. For example, in 1968 the Supreme Court overturned the "man-in-the-house" rules established in many states since 1935, which had denied benefits to mothers when an unrelated "able-bodied" male could be shown to be living with her (*King v. Smith* 1968). In 1969 eligibility was further opened up by court ruling when long-term residency requirements were found unconstitutional (*Shapiro v. Thompson* 1969). The states could no longer restrict eligibility to those who had established residence for a certain number of years, denying benefits to those suspected of having moved into a state for the purpose of collecting benefits.

Until the early seventies, grants were not "consolidated." That is, rather than offer a uniform grant to all families of the same size with the same income, most states took into consideration "special needs," for which they either paid in-kind (such as providing furniture or cribs) or by adding special needs supplements to recipients' grants. Wisconsin provided extra money for twenty-three special needs items, such as clothing for children, furniture, appliances, laundry, errands, school fees, child care, even snow shoveling (Handler and Hollingsworth 1971, p. 91).

Such grants, however, were distributed only at the discretion of caseworkers. Welfare rights advocates often alleged that such discretionary powers were abused by social workers, who supposedly bestowed extra benefits to reward compliance or withheld benefits in discriminating against minority recipients (see, e.g., Piven and Cloward 1971). At the least, some caseworkers may have been more willing to advocate for the clients than were other caseworkers, resulting in inequity in treatment. As a result, the same rules that allowed caseworkers the flexibility to recognize a particular family's special needs provoked calls for horizontal equity and uniformity.

At the same time, welfare rights leaders began using the special needs provisions as a valuable organizing tool. An organizer would assemble a group of recipients to present themselves at the local welfare office and demand furniture or clothing. Under such demands the special needs system began to break down, and most states moved to a consolidated grant, which provided uniform funds to families on the basis of family size, income, and little else.

Legal advocates, many of them employed with public funds, played an important role not only in giving momentum to the pace of change but also in defining the types of changes that were lasting. These included exhaustive objective definitions of eligibility to limit discretion and ensure horizontal equity, appeals procedures, and consolidated grants. Just as social workers had sought to reform welfare according to their own professional emphasis on casework and counseling, so too did lawyers seek to establish fair processes for eligibility determination and to ensure horizontal equity.

The Separation of Eligibility Determination and Services

One other change during the period 1967 to 1972 proved crucial to the later evolution of welfare services: the separation of eligibility determination and services. In 1967 the federal government initially issued a directive urging states to reorganize their administration of welfare, setting up separate line agencies to determine eligibility and to provide services to welfare clients and others. To speed the transition, the Bureau of Family Services (which had overseen both assistance payments and service provision for AFDC clients) was reorganized into the Social and Rehabilitation Service in 1967, setting up distinct oversight agencies for the two functions (Derthick 1975).

Separation was sought by many constituencies, each with distinct, sometimes contradictory motives. William Simon notes, "Social work lost prestige during this period as it came to be associated on the left with invasion of privacy and conformist manipulation and on the right with bleeding heart sentimentality and administrative laxity" (Simon 1983, p. 1215).

There were various reasons for the support for separation that came from within the social work community (Hoshino 1971). Many social workers were eager to shed the assistance payments function—to remove the "albatross of relief" (Hamilton 1962)—in order to have more time to provide "services." After separation, they felt they would be able to supply more services to those in need, on and off the welfare rolls. In addition, they were concerned about the inevitable perceptions of coercion by clients afraid to turn down workers' suggestions. Social workers argued that the dual role of counselor and investigator was impossible to achieve. Such perceptions of coercion, accurate or not, poisoned the "therapeutic" value of the counselor/client relationship.

Conservatives too had their reasons for supporting separation. Under Governor Ronald Reagan, California was among the first states to separate. Many were eager to see social workers—whom they perceived to be advocates—relieved of the responsibility of determining eligibility. And while many social workers saw separation as a way to expand services, conservatives, perhaps correctly, saw separation as a way to control the growth of services. Before separation, social workers themselves generated the growing demand for "hard" services with their own referrals. Once social workers were detached from the assistance function, the only demand came from those who voluntarily walked in the door. This would eventually result in a shift in social services clientele away from public assistance recipients and a slowdown in the growth of services (Piliavin and Gross 1977).

Bureaucratization and Eligibility Determination, 1972–1988

Between 1970 and 1980 the administration of AFDC was fundamentally transformed from a process characterized by discretion and a highly personalized relationship between caseworker and client into an impersonal system for verifying eligibility and writing checks. This change in mission was reflected in the manner in which local offices were organized. First, rather than continue to operate under caseloads, many local offices segmented the task of eligibility determination, specialized by function, and installed "workload" systems. Rather than see a single caseworker, a client would deal with an intake worker, a redetermination worker, a phone unit worker, a walk-in unit worker, a food stamp worker, a monthly reporting worker, and so on. Further, within each unit, work was dispensed as it presented itself. Only by chance would a client see the same redetermination worker twice. Workers were pulled out of the neighborhoods. The local welfare office became the primary locus of interaction, with department personnel doing one home visit at most, and that at the time of initiation of the grant.

Second, hiring policies evolved with the change in mission. The federally established degree requirements for new caseworkers and the caseload limits were dropped in 1969, when the focus on services was discarded. Eligibility determination, rather than needing college graduates or specialists with master's degrees in social work and counseling skills, merely required clerks to implement the eligibility criteria. Most of those with formal training in social work were transferred to newly created departments of human resources, social services, or child welfare. A Massachusetts Department of Public Welfare director of labor relations was quoted as saying, "We've been trying to get the people who think like social workers out and the people who think like bank tellers in" (Simon 1983, p. 1216). The caseworker was replaced by the "eligibility specialist" or the "eligibility technician," the new job titles reflecting the altered job definitions. The only tasks left to the welfare worker were the taking of applications, the collection of verification requirements, and the monitoring of continued eligibility.

Third, with the new preoccupation with error rates, the list of verification requirements grew dramatically, and with it so did the costs of monitoring eligibility. As late as 1969 the Department of Health, Education and Welfare had encouraged states to take clients at their word, requiring verification only when clients' self-declarations were "incomplete, unclear, or inconsistent, or . . . other circumstances in the particular case indicate to a prudent person that further inquiry should be made, and the individual cannot clarify the situation. . . ." (Simon 1983, p. 1205). In current practice, clients are expected to verify nearly every aspect of eligibility: birth certificates to verify number of children, letter from the landlord or utility bills to verify residence, wage stubs, bank statements, and so on.

Though social services and income maintenance functions had been severed in the early seventies, how the newly created state departments of public welfare would evolve was hardly inevitable. William Simon has argued that the bureaucratization of the eligibility process was due to legal rights challenges in the early seventies: restricting discretion in pursuit of horizontal equity, states developed objective definitions of eligibility based upon verifiable characteristics (Simon 1983). But there were at least two other reasons why the transformation of welfare administration took the particular direction it did. First, with 15.9 percent of all payments in Massachusetts and 26.5 percent in New York being overpayments or payments to those ineligible as late as 1973, there were many in state and local administrations eager to restore the programs' integrity by reducing the error rates (error rates from SSA–OPEQ 1980). Given tight state and local budgets, a program with high error rates was subject to across-the-board cuts. Welfare officials sought to develop objective, verifiable eligibility criteria, much like those for Social Security.

Another force giving direction to the transformation of public assistance was the federal quality control program (Gardiner and Lyman 1984). In 1970 new federal regulations required states to take samples of their active caseloads (150 in smaller states, 1,200 in states with caseloads of more than 60,000), audit the cases carefully, and compute error rates. Federal investigators in the regional offices review a smaller sample of these cases, often personally interviewing clients and other sources to verify the items of eligibility. Using data from their own investigations, federal auditors then revise the states' error rate estimates. Because the error rates become public information, state administrators can face considerable pressure from their legislators or from taxpayer groups when the error rates are high. Even without federal sanctions on states for high error rates, the federal quality control system generates pressure for lower error rates by providing ammunition to the state's critics.

The federal quality control process affected state policy in a number of ways. First, the quality control process has led to further consolidation of grants. Consolidation lowers error rates. Suppose that a state allowed for a deduction of a family's actual work-related expenses rather than setting a standard deduction for all families with earnings. Since payments were more likely to be found in error when based upon the family's reported expenses, some states adopted a standard allowance (Brodkin 1986). With the standard deduction, even if work expenses were misreported, there was no error in payment as long as the person was truly working.

Second, quality control has led the states to restrict welfare workers' discretion, specifying verification requirements in minute detail. Rather than allow workers to use their judgment in accepting adequate verification—a judgment that might differ from that of the federal reviewers, who have more time to check secondary sources—state policy manuals spell out long lists of acceptable verifications. For instance, verifying father's absence is often very difficult. The more verifications required in state manuals, the less likely federal reviewers are to find a mistake. Rather than let workers decide whether the testimony of friends or neighbors is credible, the states have specified detailed verification requirements.

This preoccupation with verification requirements is illustrated in an unreasonable attachment to written guidelines. Simon cites an example in which Cuban refugees were denied benefits for failing to provide properly certified birth certificates for their children (Simon 1983, p. 1198). He also describes a case in which a family's grant was terminated for failing to produce a recent letter verifying one child's attendance in school. Though the mother had produced similar letters in previous months, she was not able to meet the most recent request because it was August and the school was closed (Simon 1983, pp. 1198–99). The quality control review process has led to a reduction in workers' ability to exercise their own judgment.

Third, quality control focuses workers' attention on the process of eligibility determination rather than the reasonableness of clients' claims. Included in the error rate are "paper errors," such as failure to transcribe social security numbers on the application. Since such errors have no direct bearing on a client's eligibility, they further reinforce the focus on process rather than on making a reasonable personal assessment of a client's eligibility.

The states' efforts were successful. There was a dramatic decline in error rates throughout the seventies: the national average error rate fell from 16.5 percent to 7.8 percent between 1973 and 1980. Error rates have been relatively stable since 1980.[1] But as Simon observes, ". . . the transformation of the system seems to have had an important effect on the way claimants and workers experience the system and their relation to each other. The reforms seem to have reduced the claimants' experience of oppressive and punitive moralism, of invasion of privacy, and of dependence on idiosyncratic personal favor. But they also have reduced their experience of trust and personal care and have increased their experience of bewilderment and opacity" (Simon 1983, p. 1221).

Welfare Reform in the Eighties: Promoting Self-Sufficiency

The eligibility and compliance welfare system that emerged with the failure of the casework model is a system that everybody hates (Ellwood 1988). Welfare is rigid and punitive. Welfare benefits are niggardly. In many states they are so minimal that they are not sufficient to pay for basic necessities—food, clothing, shelter—on the most frugal possible budget (see Chapter 4). The casework model had held out the promise that with welfare would come social service intervention that would help recipients to correct the problems that led them to welfare in the first place. With the collapse of this model many came to see welfare as a dependency trap, in which clients received income maintenance for long periods with little hope of moving off welfare. The next two chapters show that this view of the current welfare system is a gross oversimplification, but that it contains a significant kernel of truth.

The response has been to try to make the encouragement of self-sufficiency a primary goal of welfare. During the period of change from an emphasis on social casework services to an emphasis on eligibility and compliance, several attempts were made to build expectations and requirements about self-sufficiency into the welfare system. The story of these efforts is one of conflict between the eligibility-compliance culture and the culture of self-sufficiency. With a few exceptions in selected places, requirements about work and work preparation were added on to the operating welfare system, with disappointing results for proponents of genuine cultural transformation.

Precursors of the Family Support Act

Efforts to change the welfare system's expectations about work have been made several times in the past. Until 1981, the primary mechanism for encouraging work was a system of incentives that allowed recipients to keep a portion of their earnings, without having them deducted from their grants. In 1981, efforts to cut costs and focus the program more on the "truly needy" led to the reduction of these monetary incentives and the removal of many working clients from the rolls.[2] The transition to work was to be accomplished by participation in employment activities, including work experience (workfare), which the states were encouraged to require of recipients.

Employment programs were run under the Work Incentives Program, part of the AFDC law since 1967 and until 1989 the basic program for assisting AFDC recipients to find work and leave the welfare rolls. States were required to set up programs under their state employment services. AFDC recipients with no preschool children were required to register with the WIN program, to take advantage of employment services, and to accept jobs when offered.

In 1986, 1.6 million AFDC clients were registered with the WIN program. Only about 220,000, however, were actually receiving any services, mostly assistance with job searches, and most of them under the state demonstration programs described later in this chapter. Only 130,000 WIN registrants left welfare by "working their way" off the rolls, most of them without any help from the WIN program (U.S. House, Ways and Means 1990). In most welfare offices WIN quickly became a paper compliance process, with clients and workers going through the motions of WIN registration, followed by a tacit understanding that neither the client nor the employment service was required to do much more. (The most extreme version of this attitude is apparent in the states that automated their welfare eligibility systems and programmed the computers to execute WIN registration automatically for all applicants.)

This lack of involvement of clients and workers in the WIN program came about in part because the WIN program never had enough resources available. In addition, the required coordination of welfare and employment programs was seldom managed very effectively. Welfare workers typically felt no obligation to require or encourage more active employment-directed activity. Employment service workers found welfare clients difficult to place, and saw no reason not to focus their activities on more promising clients.

There were, of course, exceptions to this general rule, offices where workers and clients were genuinely committed to preparing for and finding work. In general, however, the WIN program had little success in directing life on welfare toward a goal of self-support. WIN's fate demonstrates that legislative mandates do not necessarily lead to effective action; complying with the mandate in ways that require minimal effort and thus generate minimal results is an equally possible outcome.

Toward Self-Sufficiency: Alternative Models of Work-Welfare

In the early 1980s, a number of states established work-welfare programs aimed at correcting the shortcomings of WIN and at making serious efforts to prepare welfare clients for employment. In most cases these programs were operated by welfare departments rather than by employment services, under federal waivers of some of the WIN rules.

The well-publicized Massachusetts ET Choices Program was a voluntary program that encouraged clients to participate in education, training, and employment activities. It provided both work opportunities and supporting services, such as child care and transportation. ET appears to have brought about quite important changes in the lives of both workers and clients, and to have changed the character of their interactions. The offices looked and felt different: welfare applicants encountered job listings and recruiters in their first visit to a welfare office. Clients were assigned to a case manager who assisted them in developing a Family Independence Plan aimed at self-sufficiency. The core of the plan was a set of activities directed at employment, which could include basic education, job skills training, job search, or supported work. Child care and other services were provided as needed.

Although participation in ET was voluntary, the program was quite successful in attracting clients. A large proportion of the caseload participated in some employment-related activity. Both clients and workers saw movement to self-support as an important goal. It also appears that the daily activities of clients changed substantially under ET. Many more of them were going out to education or training, or working or looking for work, than in the typical welfare system (Nightingale et al. 1991).

Proponents of Massachusetts's ET program claimed large employment gains and welfare savings. Their claims could conceivably prove correct. But the Massachusetts caseload went down only 5 percent in the first several years of ET's existence, a drop comparable to that in other states without work-welfare programs—though also without the substantial welfare benefit increases that occurred simultaneously with ET. Especially given the great strength of the Massachusetts economy during the period that ET was implemented, the 5 percent drop in caseloads suggests that even an enthusiastically implemented and well-managed work-welfare program on this model is likely to have only a modest impact on who goes off welfare and how fast.[3]

Pre–Family Support Act work-welfare programs were also operated in other states. The Baltimore Options Program was one of the early successes. The program included job search, education, training, on-the-job training, and thirteen weeks of work experience (Gueron 1986). In this program, 28 percent of the participants were off welfare in the fifth quarter after they came on the rolls, compared with 26 percent of the control group—a positive, though hardly earth-shattering, finding. The Options Program appears to be cost-effective, under reasonable assumptions about costs and about the permanence of earnings gains. But the total net benefits amount to only about $600 per participant—modest gains, to say the least (Friedlander et al. 1985).

The most impressive gains from a work-welfare program have occurred in California's GAIN program. In one county, Riverside, the program was operated exceptionally well. The county commissioner was passionately committed to the program and set high expectations for both workers and clients. Clients were strongly encouraged to get jobs quickly, and many, though by no means all, of them did: 35 percent of the experimental group were employed at the end of two years, compared with 24 percent of the controls. The average earnings of those in the program were 50 percent higher than those of the control group, and over a two-year period they had received on average $1,400 less in welfare benefits.

Implementing the Family Support Act

The Family Support Act of 1988 is an attempt to alter the basic framework of welfare programs, mandating for all states the new emphasis on developing self-sufficiency seen in innovative state programs like ET, the Baltimore Options Program, and GAIN. The potential for changing the culture of the welfare system to one of emphasizing self-sufficiency lies in the JOBS (Job Opportunities and Basic Skills) program, which states are required to establish and recipients to participate in. In contrast to WIN, the requirement is participation, not just registration. The requirement, moreover, is extended to women whose youngest child is aged three to five as well as those whose youngest child is six or over. States must submit plans for operating programs that assess the education and training needs of clients, and provide programs and services that will enable recipients to move toward self-support. The programs must include basic skills, job skills training, and job development and placement. States are expected to provide child care and other supportive services as needed. The goal of the program is to help clients move off welfare into jobs, and to provide some transitional assistance as they establish themselves in employment.

How much change is the Family Support Act generating in the welfare system and in the lives of clients? There are, of course, issues that the act did not deal with and that therefore have not changed: the politically controversial questions of basic eligibility requirements, state variability, and welfare benefit levels.[4] The act does not modify the quality control system in any important ways, and thus state welfare systems still need to devote much of their energy to eligibility and benefit-level determination. These omissions limit the law's ability to affect the basic culture of the welfare system. What the law does include are provisions related to child support, work and training programs, and transitional assistance.

Unfortunately, the Family Support Act requirements came into effect during a very difficult time for states. During the late 1980s, a national recession led to increasing welfare caseloads and decreasing state revenues. Skyrocketing Medicaid costs and demands for prison expansion put increased demands on decreased state resources. Providing the education, employment, and training services mandated by FSA required state money (the federal government paid only about 60 percent of the cost), and the states did not have it. In 1991 the states claimed only about 60 percent of the $1 billion that the federal government had authorized for the JOBS program (Nathan 1993).

Participation rates reflected the struggles that the states had in developing JOBS programs. Under FSA states were required to exempt some recipients from participating and allowed to exempt others. In 1992 the states were exempting more than half the adult caseload, mostly mothers with children under three, but also recipients with disabilities, transportation problems, and difficulties in finding child care. Some states exempted as much as 70 or 80 percent of their caseload.

Overall, 16 percent of nonexempt AFDC recipients or 7 percent of all adult AFDC recipients were participating in JOBS programs in 1992. The best performing states reached about 15 percent of adult recipients. Some of the programs were very good. But they were a long way from achieving the goal of changing the culture or the nature of life on welfare.

ET Choices and other work-welfare programs demonstrate that under some circumstances life on welfare and in welfare offices can change quite dramatically. But dramatic change is the exception, not the rule. Several characteristics of ET seem to have been instrumental in its success and may explain what happened in other states. ET was developed and implemented at the state level, with the solid backing of the governor and the fervent commitment of an inspired welfare commissioner; it was not imposed on the state from the federal level. Management experience in both the public and the private sectors suggests that decentralized programs that are responsive to local conditions and "owned" by participants are more likely to be successful than programs imposed from the top. Clients' participation in ET was basically voluntary; though clients had to register in order to meet WIN requirements, participation in ET activities was voluntary. This meant that workers had to sell the program to clients, and thus invest themselves in its success. Workers could not get away with simply having clients fill out forms. And because the program was voluntary, clients were committed to their own success. They participated in the program because they had come to believe it could help them; this perspective seemed to make them better able to work and learn and allowed the training programs to maintain standards for attendance and participation.[5]

Another feature of ET concerned resources. Massachusetts had been willing to appropriate substantial resources for child care, training, and other services, at considerable cost; a large network of nonprofit providers of these services was already in place. The Family Support Act, in contrast, carries modest appropriations.[6] States are required to match these federal monies. Yet because of the extremely tight fiscal constraints under which most states were operating in the early 1990s, they were unable to spend even the modest amounts necessary to match the appropriations of the FSA.

This problem illustrates a more general phenomenon that limits the extent to which employment and training programs alone are likely to bring about wide-ranging changes in the welfare system. Providing employment and training services or community work experiences to welfare recipients requires investing substantial amounts of money and staff time. Such an investment can essentially double the cost of providing welfare benefits. Workfare, which involves supervision and capital costs as well as staff costs for assignment and monitoring, costs just as much. Although employment and training investments are likely to pay off in the long run, they invariably cost money in the short run—and annual state budget cycles are very short run indeed.

Because of the cost of serious employment, training, and work activities, it is not surprising that the FSA mandated relatively low participation rates, increasing from 7 percent of eligibles in 1990 to only 20 percent in 1995 (U.S. House, Ways and Means 1992, p. 614). Nor is it surprising that even states committed to a work-oriented philosophy generally have relatively low rates of actual participation.

The few exceptions to this generalization reveal another constraint on the extent to which work-welfare programs are likely to change the basic dynamics of the welfare system. ET, during the period of its success in Massachusetts in the late 1980s, and the successful examples of county GAIN programs in California operated in very tight economies with very low unemployment rates. These programs had high placement rates as well as high participation rates. In slack economies with high general unemployment rates, job placements are much more difficult. In such situations, participation requirements may actually lengthen stays on welfare, if recipients enroll in successive education or training programs. The early 1990s were years of recession and stagnant recovery, as well as fiscal crisis, in most states. These were also the first years of FSA implementation, with, not surprisingly, discouraging results.

In better economic times, states may be more willing to invest in employment and training, because they will see more tangible results more quickly. It is important, therefore, not to dismiss the potential effect of serious, large-scale employment and training programs. Nonetheless, experience with the JOBS program thus far, as with earlier employment and training efforts, underscores the inevitable limitations of such an approach taken by itself.

Truly changing the character of welfare requires genuine cultural change, reinforced by management commitment, new definitions of what welfare workers do, and adequate resources. It also requires, we believe, understanding and untangling the work-welfare dilemma, which is examined in detail in the following chapters. Changing the welfare system can only occur when life outside the welfare system also changes, so that expectations of self-sufficiency are reinforced by reality.

2

Understanding Welfare Dynamics

How long do people stay on welfare? How common are long-term stays versus short-term ones? Do people often go back on welfare once they leave, or are most departures permanent? Who are the women who stay on welfare for long periods? Who moves off more quickly? How do people leave welfare—through work, through marriage, because their children are grown? These are all fundamental questions about welfare dynamics, the answers to which can and should dramatically shape both our images of welfare and our policy responses.

If welfare is predominantly a short-term aid, with people moving quickly into private sources of support, then welfare is best understood as a transitional program. "Dependency" becomes less of a worry and policies designed to move people from welfare to work might be unnecessary, potentially even counterproductive. Relatively simple policies to help people find jobs more quickly might be as much as is needed. But if welfare lasts a very long time, then the nature and the reasons for long-term use become important, and policy responses more complex. Critical questions arise as to behavior: is long-term use a function of weak incentives to work, of a felt need to stay at home to nurture children, of illness, of a "culture of poverty" created by welfare "dependency"? Important value questions arise: is it appropriate for the government to provide an alternative source of support to paid labor market work that allows single parents to stay home, caring for their children?

28

Welfare dynamics are multifaceted, and understanding them helps explain both the heterogeneity of the welfare population and the complexity of policy solutions. We focus here on three basic questions: How long do female heads with children stay on AFDC? What are the characteristics of those who receive welfare income for relatively long versus short periods of time? How and to what do people leave welfare, and how common is moving from welfare to work? In our view, the failure to understand fully the answers to these questions often seriously distorts policy toward low-income welfare recipients.

The Duration of AFDC Use for Single Parents

One would think that the question of how long welfare lasts would have a straightforward answer. Yet consider three different answers that have appeared in one form or another in the debate over welfare policy:

- Roughly 35 percent of all current recipients have been on welfare for two years (twenty-four consecutive months) or less. Only about 20 percent have been on for ten years or more.

- Half of all spells of welfare last less than two years. Only 14 percent last ten years or more.

- Less than 15 percent of all current recipients will be on welfare for two years or less. Some 48 percent will be on in ten or more years.

The first two answers make welfare look very short lived indeed. The last answer conveys a very different impression. Remarkably, *all three are correct*. And all three come from the same set of data. Indeed the sterility of debates over welfare and the weakness of a considerable portion of welfare policies over the years can be directly traced to the inability of people to realize that all three statements capture real and important sides of welfare.

A now much-used example from outside welfare helps clear up some of the confusion. Consider the situation in a hypothetical hospital. Suppose one sat in the admitting room and observed people entering the hospital. One would quickly discover that the vast majority of those entering the hospital could expect very short stays. Most would be there for some short-term acute episode—surgery, a delivery, tests—and could be expected to leave in less than a week. Thus one could say quite legitimately that the vast majority of those beginning a hospital stay and the vast majority of people who ever enter the hospital have short stays.

But suppose one left the admitting room and walked around the hospital. One might be shocked to discover that the vast majority of beds were occupied by people with chronic conditions. Even though they were a tiny fraction of people admitted on any given day, they represented the bulk of the patients in the hospital, the bulk of the bed-days, and presumably the bulk of hospital expenditures.

The reason for the apparent paradox is easy enough to understand. One person who enters the hospital and stays for fifty-two weeks will occupy as much bed time as fifty-two people who come in for a week. Thus if every week nine acute patients enter for a one-week stay, and one chronic person enters for a fifty-two-week stay, 85 percent (52/61 total bed-weeks admitted) of the hospital beds will be filled with chronic care patients, even though they represent only 10 percent of hospital admissions (and only 10 percent of those who have ever been in the hospital).

How can we accurately describe the hospital? Only 10 percent of those who are admitted or who ever use hospital care are chronic patients, and therefore the hospital can be described as highly dynamic. Yet 85 percent of the beds, and presumably a similar portion of the expendi..ires, go to the group of chronic patients. The hospital could equally be claimed to be primarily serving a rather stagnant group.

Spell Dynamics

The analogy of the hospital fits perfectly for welfare. The vast majority of people who start on welfare will stay less than four years. Yet people who stay eight years or more account for more than half of the people on welfare at any point in time. People who stay for an extended period tend to accumulate in the system. They represent a significant portion of the caseload and of welfare expenditures, even if they are only a small fraction of those who start on welfare at any given time.

Thus one critical distinction is between durations of welfare for those *beginning* a spell on welfare and for those *on welfare at a point in time*. Table 2.1 presents data that show several different ways of describing welfare dynamics. The second and third columns (ignore the first and fourth columns for now) illustrate what a major difference looking at durations for those beginning a spell of welfare and for those on welfare at a point in time can make. We can see in column (2) that almost half of all spells for those beginning on welfare end within two years. Only 14 percent last ten years or more. (This is equivalent to looking at dynamics in the hospital admitting room.) Yet in column (3) we see that only 15 percent of people on welfare at any point in time are in the midst of a spell that will last two years or less, and 48 percent are in spells expected to last ten years or more. Both are true. Both give an accurate picture of one part of welfare.

This table is drawn from tabulations and projections using the Panel Study of Income Dynamics (PSID), the only longitudinal survey that can generate nationally representative results such as these. The PSID began with 5,000 families and single adults in 1968. Members of these original families have been followed ever since, as long as they could be found. For this analysis, we use data from the first twenty-one years of the panel study, from 1968 to 1988.[1] Because the PSID oversampled low-income households, because it collected very comprehensive annual income data, and because these households have been followed for such a long period of time, it is uniquely suitable for looking at the dynamics of AFDC receipt. For the year 1977, we did a comparison of the PSID with other data sources and found that for most purposes it is representative of the population we are interested in (Bane and Ellwood 1983).

One or two critical assumptions are built into Table 2.1, largely as a result of features of the PSID. For most of this period, the PSID asks only about annual income. Yet welfare is received monthly.

Table 2.1 Distribution of AFDC spells for female heads with children

Spell length in years	Hazard rate	Persons beginning a spell	Persons on AFDC at a point in time[b]	
	(1) Exit probability	(2) Completed spell distribution	(3) Completed spell distribution	(4) Uncompleted spell distribution
1	.31	31.0	6.6	21.3
2	.26	17.9	7.6	14.7
3	.21	10.7	6.8	10.8
4	.23	9.3	7.9	8.6
5	.18	5.6	6.0	6.6
6	.16	4.1	5.2	5.4
7	.13	2.8	4.1	4.6
8	.18	3.4	5.7	4.0
9	.07	1.1	2.0	3.2
10	.16	2.3	4.8	3.0
11	.20	2.4	5.6	2.5
12	.15	1.4	3.7	2.0
13	.19	1.5	4.3	1.7
14	.11	0.7	2.2	1.4
15	.11	0.6	2.1	1.2
16	.10	0.5	1.8	1.1
Over 16	.10[a]	4.7	23.6	7.7
Totals		100.0	100.0	100.0
Average		4.7	11.1	5.5

Source: Authors' tabulation of the 21-year Panel Study of Income Dynamics.
a. Value assumed.
b. Derived from column (2) assuming no-growth steady state.

People can be on one month and off the next. We cannot observe monthly dynamics. We classify a person as having received AFDC in a year if they got benefits that exceed the maximum allowed for a single month in their state. Thus a "spell" of AFDC might actually be a string of years in which the person received AFDC in some months each year, but not for every month. Our spells are best understood as consecutive years in which the person reported receiving AFDC.

Others have used monthly data to look at dynamics, and not surprisingly, when spells are measured as continuous months of welfare, they are shorter. Whereas we show that 49 percent receive welfare at some point in no more than two consecutive years, researchers using monthly data often find that no more than 30 percent receive welfare in twenty-four consecutive months. Still, the monthly data can be quite misleading. Many people leave welfare for only a month or two and return later. For example, LaDonna Pavetti (1993) found that 70 percent of younger women who left welfare in some month returned for another episode. Some of these short exits are simply administrative churning—caused by the failure of the recipient to meet some administrative rule, which leads to a termination that is followed by a return to welfare as soon as the rule is met. In other cases, the person does get a short-term job. But for whatever reason, these individuals do not leave welfare permanently.

Thus annual data tend to knock out short-lived exits and returns, and that offers some advantages. Few would classify a person who left welfare for only a month or two as really having escaped it. Nevertheless, annual data can obscure some of the more rapid moves on and off welfare, a point we shall return to shortly.

Contrasting monthly and annual data points out a problem in any spell analysis: people may have more than one spell. Often it is total time on welfare which is of interest, not the duration of a single episode. We turn to that issue shortly. In any case, we have no choice but to use annual data for this analysis.

Another limitation is that we are forced to look at some people who started welfare a rather long time ago. Only people who started welfare at least ten years ago can provide information on spells lasting a decade or more. If the rules for receipt or the behavior of recipients changed radically over time, one might get a misleading impression. In fact, we see little evidence that the basic pattern of welfare dynamics has changed much in the past ten to fifteen years (largely because of offsetting changes in rules and the population on welfare).

The final assumption in the "point in time" estimates is that we are in "steady state." In this context the term means that the same number of people are entering welfare each year and have been doing so throughout the past. If there were a sudden rise in new entrants because of a temporary dip in the economy, the caseload would temporarily have a larger fraction of short-term recipients. By contrast, an economic boom would tend to draw off short-term recipients more quickly, leaving only longer-term recipients on the program. Thus the point in time estimates should be seen as the overall tendency, not a perfect reflection of the current caseload.

Returning to the first column of Table 2.1, we find the "exit rate" or what is sometimes called the "hazard rate" from AFDC. The basic building block on which the entire table is built, it shows the probability a person who has already been on welfare for the time shown will stop receiving welfare during that year. The .31 in the top row of the first column shows the probability that a person who receives welfare in one year will exit welfare and not receive it in the next. Thus this column shows the rate at which people are leaving welfare after being on for a given number of years.

Exit rates tell an important story. They are indicators of whether people become more or less likely to leave AFDC as spell durations rise. We find that exit rates are almost always higher in the first few years, falling off in later years. The pattern is particularly pronounced for those who have been on more than two years.

The decline in the exit rate after the first few years could occur for two conceptually very distinct reasons. It could be that the AFDC population is very heterogeneous from the start. Some have skills, ability, or the motivation to leave quickly. Others find it harder to exit. In the early years, when a larger fraction of fast exiters are in the mix, the exit rates look high. In later years, the slower exiters are left behind. Thus the average exit rate falls. No one changes while on welfare, but a different mix of people are on for one year than are on for, say, five years, so the average exit rate falls.

Conversely, welfare may, indeed, alter behavior. People who might have gotten off more readily at first could become conditioned by welfare and have a harder time leaving it after being on a few years. In that case, people change while on the rolls. The decline in average exit probabilities would then reflect declines in individual exit probabilities as people stay on welfare.

In the next chapter we examine these differing explanations. But regardless of the explanation, for policy purposes, the first two years do seem important. Many recipients will leave during this period. Those who remain after two years are much more likely to be long-term recipients either because of personal characteristics or because of behavioral changes.

Before examining the fourth column of Table 2.1, let us first briefly return to the hospital example. Suppose that instead of asking how long people in the beds will eventually spend in the hospital, we asked how long people have been there since they were admitted. We would be asking about *uncompleted spell* durations. Such a question is very easy to answer using administrative data. All one has to do is look at the date the person was admitted and tabulate the time in the hospital so far. Unfortunately, this information is not very useful. Worse, it can give a highly misleading picture of dynamics. If we ask how many of the current patients have already stayed in the hospital a long time, the number will be much smaller than if we ask how many of the current patients will eventually stay a long time. A newly admitted chronic patient has only been in the hospital a short time. But it certainly is not sensible to classify him or her as a short-term patient.

Until very recently the most common way of describing welfare dynamics by program administrators was with uncompleted spell durations. In our view, uncompleted spell durations are of very limited value when seeking to understand welfare dynamics. They are almost always misleading, except for a very limited set of policy questions. Consider for example what would happen if there were a sudden increase in the number of women who had children out of wedlock and entered welfare. Initially uncompleted durations would go down, because these new recipients would have only recently enrolled in the program. But as later results illustrate, it would be a terrible mistake to conclude that welfare spells were now shorter. In reality, most unmarried mothers will eventually have relatively long durations.

The uncompleted spell durations are still widely used for a very simple reason. They sound sensible initially, and they are the sole measure of dynamics that is very easy to produce. Administrators need only look at their current caseload and see how long each person has been on. It is impossible to look at the current caseload and determine with certainty how long each person will eventually be on welfare. Until the spell is over we cannot be sure how long it will last. Thus to determine how many people currently on welfare are in the midst of a very long spell of welfare, we generally have to make projections. These can be made on the basis of information on uncompleted spells, used in conjunction with information on the experiences of past recipients and making certain assumptions. That is what was done to produce column (3) in Table 2.1. But case studies of current recipients or program data alone cannot provide information on completed spell durations without fairly sophisticated statistical inferences. Thus, for most purposes, we believe uncompleted spell durations should not be used at all.

Table 2.1 makes clear one critical insight: the welfare population is heterogeneous. The vast majority of people starting welfare at a point in time and the vast majority of people who ever have spells on welfare stay only a short time. Yet the majority of welfare recipients at a point in time are in the midst of a much longer spell, and most welfare funds are spent on them.

These findings have critical policy significance. They suggest that welfare is not a drug that ensnares the vast majority of people who ever avail themselves of welfare support. For most, welfare is a short-term transitional program. But for a smaller number, spells can be quite long. And these long-termers represent a very large portion of the recipients at any one time. Because long-term recipients are a large portion of the caseload, they receive a roughly equivalently large portion of the dollars we spend on welfare. This finding has strong implications for programs that seek to invest resources for the training or education of recipients with the goal of moving them off of welfare. A strategy of heavy investment in all new welfare recipients will lead to the bulk of expenditures going to people who would have left quickly anyway. Such investments might be seen as inefficient. By contrast, a policy that effectively targeted resources on persons who would otherwise become long-term recipients and moved them off more quickly could yield a high payoff, even if considerable resources were expended.

Welfare Returns and Total Time on Welfare

Thus far we have talked about distinctions between (a) durations for those beginning a spell and for those on welfare at a point in time, and (b) uncompleted and completed spell durations. There is a third, even more important, conceptual distinction: *spells* versus *total time* on welfare. Many women who leave welfare do not do so permanently.

Table 2.2 shows the return rate to welfare and cumulative fraction of women who have returned within a given period of time using the PSID annual data. Recall that to leave welfare in these data a woman must report no welfare for at least one year. Yet even after being off for a year, a significant number return. Seventeen percent who get off of welfare report receiving it again the following year. Cumulatively after six years, 32 percent of those who leave welfare will have returned. Note the pattern of return rates. Recidivism is much more common in the first couple of years. Women who stay off welfare for three years are relatively unlikely to return. Keeping someone off of welfare for several years may be the key to preventing a recurrence.

In part, the high return rate observed here may be caused by some sample members' failing to report AFDC income in a given year, thereby falsely creating the appearance of recidivism. A second potential explanation for the high measured recidivism is that some persons push their income above the AFDC benefit levels by such small margins that even minor setbacks push them back on the rolls. Average incomes for single mothers who were formerly on welfare tend to be low. Yet average nonwelfare income is considerably higher in the years between welfare episodes for those who do return to AFDC. Nonwelfare income rises sharply from the final year of the spell to the first year off of AFDC, and then falls sharply again as the recipient returns to AFDC. Thus while recidivism is partially a phenomenon of women who have never achieved real

Table 2.2   Estimates of rates of return to welfare, and cumulative
percentage of persons who return to AFDC by number of years
since last receiving AFDC

Number of years since last receiving AFDC	Proportion who return to AFDC[a]	Cumulative percentage of former AFDC recipients who return to AFDC
1	.17	17
2	.07	23
3	.05	26
4	.03	29
5	.03	31
6	.02	32
7	.01	33
8	.04	35
Over 8	.00	35

Source: Authors' tabulation of the 21-year Panel Study of Income Dynamics.
a. These figures are the proportion of women still off AFDC at the end of the
previous year who returned to AFDC in the indicated year.

independence from welfare and then return to it, a considerable
proportion reflects significant changes in family and economic circumstances.

Recidivism is even more pronounced when one uses monthly
data. We noted above that spells defined by monthly data are shorter
than those from annual data. Not surprisingly, monthly data also
reveal much higher rates of welfare return. As already noted, Pavetti
(1993) found that over 70 percent return to welfare eventually after
leaving it for a month.

The pattern of welfare returns highlights the limitation of looking
only at a single spell of welfare receipt when examining welfare
dynamics. This problem is especially great if one is using monthly
data, but it applies also to annual data. By looking only at the
duration of a single spell of welfare, one ignores the fact that the
recipient may have previously been on welfare or that she may use

it again after the current spell ends. For many purposes, we care far less about continuous periods of welfare receipt (spells) and more about the total time a person will have in multiple spells.

We might now ask, for those people starting a *first* spell of AFDC, what is the *total time* they will be on welfare in one or multiple spells. For those on welfare at a point in time, we might similarly ask about the total time they will eventually spend on welfare. Such a calculation is quite complex, but with certain assumptions it can be done. Using PSID data, we were able to project the number of years a single mother would receive AFDC in total over a hypothetical twenty-five-year period that began with her initial entry into AFDC (see Table 2.3). Because of the many assumptions needed to generate this table, the results should be treated with caution. They do

Table 2.3 Percentage distribution of the expected total time on AFDC for first-time female AFDC recipients and for all women receiving AFDC at a point in time

Expected total time on AFDC	Women beginning a first spell of AFDC	Women receiving AFDC at any point in time
1 year	20.9	3.4
2 years	15.6	5.1
3 years	10.0	4.8
4 years	8.6	5.6
5 years	6.2	5.0
6 years	5.5	5.3
7 years	4.3	4.8
8 years	3.7	4.8
9 years	3.2	4.6
10 or more years	22.1	56.6
Total	100.0	100.0
Average years of receipt	6.2	12.0

Source: Authors' tabulation of the 21-year Panel Study of Income Dynamics.

give our best estimate of the dynamics of welfare when multiple spells are counted.

Table 2.3 shows total time durations on welfare for those beginning a first spell and for those on at a point in time. The pattern is similar to that of Table 2.1, but durations are noticeably longer. Now only 36 percent (rather than 49 percent) of people beginning a first spell will be on for two years or less, and over half of those women receiving welfare at any point in time are in the midst of spells lasting ten years or more.

From the data in Table 2.3, welfare starts to look quite long indeed. The vast majority (81 percent) of current recipients are in the midst of total welfare times that will last five years or more. Fifty-seven percent will be on in ten or more years. Long-term use of welfare is a very real and potentially quite costly phenomenon.

Yet to interpret Table 2.3 as showing a much less dynamic pattern than Table 2.1 is a mistake. The table still shows that less than one quarter of those starting on welfare will actually collect welfare in ten different years. And recall that the table links together multiple episodes of welfare to create a total time measure. Behind the total time may be multiple episodes on and off welfare. Pavetti's (1993) work makes this especially clear. She finds that almost 90 percent of mothers who enter welfare before age twenty-four will leave at least briefly during the forty-eight months after they first go on welfare. But the vast majority who exit then return. She finds that total time calculations such as ours, which are based on annual data, seem to give a relatively accurate impression about total times on welfare, but that they miss considerable monthly dynamics.

Short-termers, Long-termers, and Cyclers

Over the years we have consistently emphasized the dual nature of welfare receipt. For many, welfare serves as short-term transitional assistance. For others it is long-term income support. It is the latter group that is often labeled "welfare dependent." In recent years our thinking has changed in one important aspect. We now believe that our thinking about long-term recipients has been too unidimensional. Many of the long-termers would be better labeled "cyclers":

people who move on and off welfare, apparently trying to leave, but unable to do so permanently.

Research suggests that these cyclers are people who have tried to leave welfare, often repeatedly, but who seem unable to maintain full independence. They obtain a job or find additional support elsewhere, but the improvement is only temporary. Their child becomes ill or they miss a day of work, and they are back on welfare. Some of the cycling, as already noted, is caused by administrative actions. People who fail to comply with department rules, such as providing key information or appearing for a redetermination visit, are often cut off from welfare until they conform, creating a kind of false dynamics.

An important fraction of those whom we might initially have classified as long-termers appear to be cyclers. Comparing the total time with the spell durations already indicates that many people with long total times have multiple spells. The high rates of recidivism in our data and the extraordinary rates of exits and returns in monthly data strongly suggest at least a subgroup that is a highly dynamic population, even among the longer-term recipients. Thus welfare has at least three sides: transitional support, episodic support, and long-term continuous support.

The recognition that long-termers are actually a heterogeneous and often relatively dynamic group is very important for policymakers. For if most people leave welfare, only to fall back into it, then perhaps the focus of policy ought to be not only on getting people off but also on making it possible for people to stay off. Cycling deserves much more attention. Why do so many people who try to exit welfare fail to leave permanently? What can and should policy do to make more exits permanent ones? More research is needed, using monthly instead of annual data, to make cycling better understood.

Dynamics, Press, and Policy

Since we first generated our estimates of welfare spell durations, the press has carried numerous reports on welfare and cited all sorts of figures on dynamics. They have been used in public debate and policy discussions. Yet all too often only one dimension of welfare is highlighted. The complexity of describing dynamics effectively, coupled with any writer's or speaker's desire to emphasize one side of welfare or another all too often lead him or her to pick one figure or another. The only fair reading of welfare recognizes all three dimensions. Many recipients stay on welfare only a short time. Most of the dollars go to people who do stay a long time. Some people go off quickly, some people go on and off repeatedly, some stay on almost continuously.

Welfare is definitely not as dynamic as some liberal advocates argue. Those who use uncompleted, monthly spell durations for current recipients create the impression that almost no one is on welfare for a long time. Uncompleted spell durations are a highly questionable and generally quite misleading indicator of dynamics. Similarly, in opposition to assertions by conservatives, there is little in these data to support the notion that welfare is a narcotic that traps most of its users. Welfare does not typically become a permanent way of life in which recipients make few efforts to escape and remain on welfare for generations.

Like so much of social policy, the picture is complicated. But complexity can be helpful. Instead of suggesting that welfare is a hopeless morass with few avenues for policy, the very heterogeneity of the population suggests that a more differentiated set of policies might effectively be used. But that requires a deeper look into the dynamics of welfare, the characteristics of long-term recipients, and the role of work and other factors in moving people off of welfare.

What Factors Are Associated with Longer Durations and Recidivism?

The natural first step in understanding long-term welfare receipt is to ask which characteristics seem to be associated with longer stays on welfare. We begin by asking: holding all else the same, what is the impact of education or race or marital status or some other variable on welfare durations and recidivism?

We estimated a series of statistical models that allow us to determine the marginal impact of various characteristics. We generated estimates separately for first spells, for returns to welfare, and for later spells. We had a sample from PSID that included 1,000 women who began a first spell, 1,438 who ended a first or later spell and could have returned, and 549 women who began a second spell. In the analyses of first and subsequent spells of AFDC receipt, all explanatory variables were measured at the start of the AFDC spell. In the analysis of recidivism, all variables were measured in the first year after the persons left AFDC, except for marital status, which was measured at the end of the previous spell.[2] We experimented with several estimation methods and ultimately used a binomial logit model because of its simplicity, though other hazard model methods yielded remarkably similar results. The methodology is summarized in the Appendix.

The actual coefficients (reported in the Appendix) indicating the impact of various factors are difficult to interpret directly. Thus we have converted the information into a form that is easier to interpret. The estimates of impacts were calculated by comparing hypothetical persons who have mean values for all characteristics except the one characteristic whose effect is being assessed. We then predicted for that hypothetical person what her expected duration of a first spell would be, what the odds were that she would return to AFDC after leaving the first spell, and what the duration of a second spell would be if she did return. In effect, we held all characteristics constant except the one being considered and calculated expected durations and the chances of a return to welfare. Because the method asks only about the effect of changing one characteristic at the margin, we labeled these results "marginal" impacts. Table 2.4 shows the marginal impact of various factors.

The table demonstrates the sensitivity of both the duration of spells and the odds of recidivism to these variations in particular characteristics. The first line of the table suggests that, if one were to examine persons who exhibited the average characteristics of the sample, the predicted average duration of first spells would be 4.4 years, the probability of having a repeat spell would be 44.6 percent, and the average duration of repeat spells would be 3.3 years.

The results suggest that five characteristics have especially strong relationships with welfare dynamics: race, education, marital status, work experience, and disability status all influence first-spell dura-

Table 2.4 Ceteris paribus estimates of the duration of AFDC receipt and the likelihood of recidivism associated with AFDC recipient characteristics

Recipient characteristics at time of beginning spell	Average duration of first spell (years)	Percentage who return to AFDC	Average duration of repeat spells (years)
All	4.4	44.6	3.3
Age			
Under 22	4.4	54.9	5.7
22–30	4.6	52.9	4.4
31–40	4.8	39.7	3.0
Over 40	3.8	39.1	2.5
Race			
White	3.5	32.3	3.5
Black	4.8	48.2	3.4
Other	3.8	41.6	3.0
Education			
High school graduate	3.6	39.2	3.1
High school dropout	5.3	51.0	3.5
Marital Status			
Never married	6.1	50.6	3.0
Married	1.7	42.6	1.4
Divorced	3.3	40.6	3.5
Widowed	2.0	43.2	2.8
Separated	4.8	44.1	4.2
Disability Status			
Disabled	6.2	46.2	3.4
Not disabled	4.1	44.2	3.3
Age of Youngest Child			
Under 3 years	4.6	36.8	2.9
3–5 years	4.6	48.9	3.1
6–10 years	4.0	53.9	3.4
Over 10 years	3.4	45.3	4.0
Number of Children			
0–1	4.3	35.7	3.2
2–3	4.4	53.7	3.3
Over 3	4.8	46.0	3.6
Work Experience			
No recent work	5.5	49.0	3.3
Recent work	4.0	42.2	3.3

Source: These figures are based on logit models estimated on the 21-year Panel Study of Income Dynamics. They assume that individuals have the sample mean values of all characteristics, except those indicated by the row descriptor.

tions. These same variables generally have a substantial influence on recidivism as well.

Other things equal, it is estimated that women who have never been married at the time they begin their first spell of AFDC will have a longer than average first-spell duration (6.1 years, on average), will be more likely to return to welfare (50.6 percent), and will have a duration of repeat spells at about the average (3.0 years). Education also is important. Lower levels of education are associated with longer durations of first spells of AFDC receipt and a greater likelihood of recidivism.

Most of these findings are not particularly surprising. One would expect dropouts, teen mothers, and women with limited work experience to have more trouble in the labor market. Still, it is somewhat more surprising that never-married mothers are less likely to leave welfare and more likely to return once they do depart. Marital status per se would not necessarily influence a single mother's chances in the labor market. But as we shall see shortly, work is not the only route out of welfare. Marriage and reconciliation are often even more common than work. Evidence to be discussed will indicate that never-married mothers are much less likely to leave welfare for marriage or other nonwork reasons than are other women. Those differences account for an important part of never-married mothers' longer durations on welfare.

The most notable aspect of the estimates by race/ethnicity group is that the differences among groups are relatively modest when all else is held equal. African-Americans with mean characteristics for the entire sample are predicted to have first spells lasting a little more than a year longer than those for whites. There is little difference in the length of repeat spells, though the recidivism rate is somewhat higher. African-American AFDC recipients are more likely than white recipients to have low levels of education, to be single, and to have large families—all factors that are positively associated with welfare dependence. Thus, as we shall see when all other factors are not held constant, African-Americans typically have much longer spells than whites. Still, it is noteworthy that the impact of race per se is quite modest after controlling for other factors.

One surprise for us is the relative impotence of certain variables, especially the age of the youngest child and the age of the recipient. We anticipated that the age of the recipient's youngest child would have a large impact, yet there is little evidence here that the age of the youngest child has an important influence on spell durations or recidivism.[3] We interpret these results as suggesting that good reasons exist to offer remedial services to women, regardless of the ages of their children. The young mother is stereotypically viewed as someone who is likely to become trapped on welfare. We found little evidence that age alone or the age of the youngest child alone increases dependence. All else is rarely held constant, however. Young mothers are more likely than average to be single, and they tend to have less work experience than average. In a later section we will see that when all else is not held equal these factors are very important predictors of total welfare time.

The most consistent patterns of impact on the three measures of welfare dynamics pertain to previous work experience and disability status. Other things being equal, both disability and less work experience are associated with much higher than average durations of first spells of AFDC receipt and with above-average probabilities of recidivism.

One other surprise appeared in our data. Essentially nothing predicts durations of later spells. Factors such as race and education work well in explaining first durations, but people who come back for repeat spells seem far less influenced by these factors. It may be that those who slip back into welfare get discouraged, or that those who do come back are more disadvantaged in ways that we were unable to measure.

Presumably a major reason for seeking to understand the nature of long-term dependency is to do something about it. We saw earlier that some persons are short-term recipients, others much longer. If one could identify likely long- and short-term recipients immediately upon their entry into welfare, one might concentrate or target education, training, and employment strategies on the prospective long-termers. Indeed, because long-termers stay so long, one can justify much larger expenditures for them if the program is successful in moving them off welfare relatively quickly, since they otherwise would receive a great deal in public aid.

Who are the long-term recipients? Are they unmarried mothers? Women with limited education? The results described so far only tell the effect of an individual characteristic at the margin. We know that never-married women are somewhat less likely to leave AFDC than are divorced and separated women if all else is the same. But never-married women are not typically the same as other recipients. They tend to have less education, less work experience, be younger themselves, and have younger children than divorced and separated mothers.

For many purposes, policymakers need information on the characteristics of different groups when all else is not held constant. If administrators are considering targeting intensive interventions on women with less work experience, they need to know what fraction of the beginning caseload has limited work experience, what proportion they are of the overall caseload, and what fraction will be long-term recipients. If women with less work experience typically have many other characteristics that tend to increase durations, such a strategy might make very good sense. If women with limited work experience often have other characteristics that tend to help them leave welfare earlier, however, it may not make sense to target there. In effect one needs information about the size and dynamics of particular subgroups of recipients.

In order to estimate the overall welfare dynamics for subgroups, we selected all persons in the subgroup who started a first spell of AFDC at some time during the 1980–1988 period in the sample from the PSID. For each individual in that subgroup, we predicted her pattern of dynamics based on her particular characteristics using the statistical models whose results were summarized earlier. We were able to predict these recipients' odds of having a one year, two year, or some other length first spell. We looked at their odds of recidivism. We calculated the expected length of subsequent spells. We also predicted the fraction of the overall caseload that people with these characteristics would represent if the mix of people entering welfare remained unchanged for an extended period (steady state). We then aggregated across all persons in a particular subgroup.

For example, to compare the aggregate welfare dynamics of blacks and whites when everything else is not held equal, we have predicted future welfare dynamics for all whites and for all blacks in the PSID sample and summarized the results for each group. We have labeled the result of this exercise "aggregate or group" information, to distinguish it from the "marginal" impacts already presented.[4]

Readers should be aware that these results are based on statistical predictions. They are somewhat sensitive to assumptions and specifications. They require long-term projections. They implicitly assume that the rules of AFDC remain unchanged and that the economy is stable. Thus all these results should be treated as tendencies and hypothetical predictions of what will happen if the future is like the past.

The results are reported in Table 2.5, which shows different distribution and duration information for different ways of dividing the sample into subgroups. For example, if one divides the sample into age groups, one finds that 29.4 percent of persons who began a spell of welfare during the 1980–1988 period were under twenty-two years of age when they began. But in steady state (if the entering case mix remained unchanged for an extended period) this group would be 37 percent of all recipients. They stay on welfare an average of nearly 7.8 years, and 31.3 percent are expected to be long-term recipients. Thus a plan to target young mothers as they enter AFDC would serve 29 percent of the new entrants and 37 percent of the eventual caseload.

Women who began when they were thirty-one to forty or over forty, by contrast, were predicted to stay on AFDC an average of less than five years, and no more than 14 percent of the group were expected to stay for ten years or more.

Looking down the last two columns of Table 2.5 makes it easy to pinpoint subgroups that have particularly long or short durations. Looking at the first two columns helps give a sense of the fraction of people involved. Clearly durations vary widely by groups. Five subgroupings seem to have the greatest risk of long durations: women who enter AFDC as teenagers, blacks, high school dropouts, never-married mothers, and women who have no recent work experience.

If we seek to reduce long-term welfare use, some of these groups

Table 2.5 Percentage of AFDC recipients with various characteristics and average total duration of AFDC receipt: Aggregate or group results for single characteristics

Recipient characteristics at time of beginning first spell	Percentage of all first-time recipients (new beginnings)	Percentage of recipients at any point in time[a]	Percentage who will have AFDC spells of 10 years or more
Age			
Under 22	29.4	37.0	31.3
22–30	51.1	47.8	20.0
31–40	11.0	8.4	13.4
Over 40	8.5	6.8	14.1
Race			
White	60.1	48.0	15.0
Black	35.7	47.5	33.7
Other	4.1	4.5	25.4
Education			
High school graduate	57.5	46.5	15.2
High school dropout	42.5	53.5	31.3
Marital Status			
Never married	42.6	55.0	32.3
Married	6.7	2.5	0.5
Divorced	24.3	17.7	12.5
Widowed	3.9	2.2	6.6
Separated	22.5	22.6	22.2
Disability Status			
Disabled	18.2	17.3	20.3
Not disabled	81.8	82.7	22.5
Age of Youngest Child			
Under 3 years	65.1	69.6	24.5
3–5 years	17.7	17.4	21.7
6–10 years	13.8	10.9	14.5
Over 10 years	3.4	2.0	7.8
Number of Children			
0–1	59.7	57.9	21.0
2–3	37.3	38.1	22.9
Over 3	3.0	3.9	32.5
Work Experience			
No recent work	22.8	29.3	31.9
Recent work	77.2	70.7	19.2

Source: Authors' tabulation of the 21-year Panel Study of Income Dynamics.
a. These figures assume that the AFDC caseload is in a "steady state."

must be targeted. But we do not necessarily have to target them all, because the groups are overlapping. Many teenagers entering AFDC are also single mothers, dropouts, and have little work experience. Indeed, it is precisely because teen mothers are more likely to be never married with limited educations that they tend to have longer durations on AFDC. It appears that our results are driven mainly by three factors: marital status, education, and work experience. When other groupings yield longer durations, it is because these subgroups have a disproportionate share of people who have never married, who have dropped out, or who have limited work experience.

For example, even though race and mother's age had relatively little impact when all else was held constant, when one does not hold all else equal, African-American women and teen mothers who started on AFDC in the 1980s have much longer durations than do others. The single biggest reason is that these groups are far more likely to be never married than others in the sample are.

This difference between marginal and average results also shows up for age of youngest child. And again the reason is that mothers with younger children are more likely to be never married. Still, the differences by age of children are smaller than those for other groupings. Grouping mothers by age of child at the beginning has less impact than grouping by education, work experience, or marital status.

One big surprise is that grouping people by disability status has little impact on predicted durations. In part this reflects the fact that disabled persons often have other attributes that enhance their ability to leave welfare. And in part this probably also reflects the tendency of the most disabled persons to leave AFDC and instead receive benefits under the Social Security or Supplemental Security programs for disabled adults. This result and any possible policy implications drawn from it should be treated with great caution. First, disability in our data is self-reported. The reliability of this information is uncertain at best (although the variable did perform reasonably well in our marginal results). Second, the impact of disability is quite sensitive to specification. If we include current disability status at each year in the spell, rather than disability status only at the beginning of the spell, it appears to be a much stronger predictor of long welfare stays.

There are dramatic differences in welfare durations of various subgroups. Some groups are three or more times more likely to have long stays on welfare. At the same time, even among the subgroups that have the longest durations, the vast majority of new entrants do not stay more than ten years. In none of the subgroups shown here do we predict that more than one third of the entering cohort will be long-term recipients. Thus even when looking at total welfare time, and even when examining these subgroupings, long-term welfare receipt is still very much the exception.

We also need to remember the importance of considering those beginning welfare versus those on welfare at a point in time. Overall, only 22 percent of those beginning a first spell stay for ten years, but that group represents 57 percent of recipients on welfare at a point in time. Similarly, even though only 32 percent of never-married mothers who begin on welfare will stay for ten years, we calculate that 66 percent of never-married mothers on welfare at a point in time are in the midst of total welfare time of ten years or more. The never-married mothers who move off more slowly tend to accumulate and become a much larger fraction of the overall caseload.

Thus far, we have looked at subgroups in which people are classified only by a single characteristic, such as marital status or education. We might instead group people by several variables. For example, we could look at never-married mothers who dropped out of school. Table 2.6 shows a breakdown by both marital status and education. Here even sharper differences emerge.

Nineteen percent of women entered AFDC as never married, without a high school diploma. These women were expected to stay an average of over ten years, and 44.6 percent were predicted to stay past ten years. Even though they were less than one fifth of the new entrants, they eventually became nearly one third of the ongoing AFDC caseload. At the other extreme are women who began as formerly married with at least a high school diploma. These women were 34 percent of the entering cohort, and were expected to have

Table 2.6   Percentage of AFDC recipients with various characteristics and average total durations of AFDC receipt: Aggregate subgroup results

Recipient characteristics at time of beginning first spell	Percentage of all first-time recipients (new beginnings)	Percentage of recipients at any point in time[a]	Average number of years of AFDC receipt	Percentage who will have AFDC spell of 10 or more years
Marital and Education Status				
Never married and high school dropout	19.1	31.2	10.1	44.6
Never married and high school graduate	23.4	23.8	6.3	22.2
Ever married and high school dropout	23.3	22.3	5.9	20.5
Ever married and high school graduate	34.1	22.7	4.1	10.5
Experience and Education Status				
No recent work and high school dropout	12.3	19.2	9.6	41.2
No recent work and high school graduate	10.5	10.2	6.0	20.9
Recent work and high school dropout	30.2	34.4	7.0	27.3
Recent work and high school graduate	47.1	36.3	4.8	14.0

Source: Simulation model estimates are based on the 21-year Panel Study of Income Dynamics.
a. These figures assume that the AFDC caseload is in a "steady state."

average durations of only four years, with only about 10 percent remaining for ten years.

We can, of course, break things down still further. If we look at never-married mothers who have not completed high school and who have no work experience, we find that over half will stay more than ten years and that the average duration reaches nearly twelve years. But this group represents only 8 percent of the entering cohort (14 percent of the caseload) so the sample sizes get quite small.

This information provides a strong indication of who the long-term recipients of AFDC are. Ultimately, though, to provide aid, we need to understand far more about what brings people to welfare and how and why some are able to leave while others are not.

The Beginnings of Welfare

Because we know the years in which welfare spells begin and end, we can try to determine which events seem to lead to welfare entries and exits. Combining data across years, we attempted to identify and classify the major events associated with the entries and exits we observed.[5]

Given the complexity of people's lives and the tendency for many things to happen at once, why someone entered or left welfare is not always easy to decide, especially on the basis of survey data. After considerable experimentation we developed a procedure that classified beginning events. To determine why people came on welfare, our procedure looked first for family structure changes that would have created categorical eligibility for the basic AFDC program. We looked for family structure changes both in the year the spell began and in the previous year. If such a change was found, it was classified as the reason for beginning welfare. If no such changes were found, we next looked for decreases in non-AFDC income of at least $500 (in constant 1978 dollars).[6] If no income decreases of this magnitude were found, we looked first to see whether the family had grown in the past year, creating the need for additional income. (Note, however, that the arrival of a first child to a female head would be classified as a categorical relationship change.) Next we looked to see whether the family had moved between counties in the past year. If none of these changes was found, the beginning was classified as unexplained.

Table 2.7 presents the distribution of reasons for people begin-

Table 2.7   Percentage distribution for beginning types for first spells of AFDC

Beginning type	Percentage of all beginnings
Wife became female head	42.1
Unmarried woman[a] without child became female head with child	38.8
Female head's earnings fell	7.1
Other	
Fall in other's earnings	2.0
Fall in other income	3.2
Family size grew	2.5
Moved	0.2
Unidentified	4.0
Total	100.0

Source: Authors' tabulation of the 21-year Panel Study of Income Dynamics.
a. Unmarried women include those who are single, divorced, widowed, or separated.

ning a first spell of welfare over the entire period of our sample. Simply put, AFDC spells almost always begin with a relationship change. Over 40 percent begin when a wife becomes a female head. Another 39 percent start when a never-married, divorced, or separated woman (a group we sometimes refer to collectively as "unmarried") gives birth to, adopts, or brings home from somewhere else ("acquires") a child.[7] Only 7 percent begin after a decrease in earnings. These women did not become female family heads in the year they began AFDC or in the year prior, but they began to receive AFDC income when their incomes fell. The other recipients are scattered across other categories.

That so few spells of AFDC begin with earnings changes suggests that a female household head does not typically go on AFDC for the first time because she has lost her job, reduced her hours, or experienced a drop in wages. These changes undoubtedly occur, but they are not usually the reasons that women begin a first spell of welfare receipt.

These results lead to a critical conclusion: prevention is the best cure. Welfare use begins because single-parent families are formed. If we could prevent the formation of new single-parent families, we could largely eliminate the need for AFDC. Yet although some efforts have been made in the past to reduce the formation of single-parent families, the number of such families continues to grow. Most disturbingly of all, the proportion of children born out of wedlock continues to rise rapidly. Absent an ability to change family formation and dissolution patterns dramatically, we will be forced to rely on methods to help single parents move off of welfare if the goal is to reduce long-term welfare use.

Exits from Welfare and the Role of Work

For welfare exits, we created a classification scheme similar to the one for welfare beginnings. Like the one for beginnings, the system is hierarchical. It begins by looking for events that caused a female household head with a child to cease being so classified and thus lose eligibility for AFDC. If she married, remarried, or reconciled so that she was no longer classified as a female household head in our data, the ending was attributed to "becoming a wife" (for lack of a better term). If a female household head with children ceased to have any children living with her, either because all the children moved out or because they had all reached their nineteenth birthday and were no longer classified as children, the exit was labeled "no longer had an eligible child."

If the woman remained a household head after leaving welfare, the procedure looked for a reasonably large change (over $500 in 1978 dollars) in income other than welfare that might explain the departure. If such a change was found, the component of income (head's earnings, the earnings of others, or other transfers) that had the largest change was designated the primary reason for departure. Thus if there was a substantial earnings change, and if the person remained a household head with a child, then her exit was classified as an earnings exit. If no major income change was found, we looked for a family size change or for a move between states. If none of these changes had occurred, the reason for leaving welfare was classified as unidentified.

The results of this classification system of exits are shown in Table 2.8.[8] Some 29 percent who left welfare became a wife; 11 percent left when they no longer had eligible children. Only 25 percent of exits could be unambiguously traced to an earnings increase using this classification system. Other transfer income increases (perhaps moving to other programs such as Social Security Disability or Supplementary Security Income) accounted for 12 percent of exits. The rest were scattered across other types of exits or unidentified.

When we first saw these results we were surprised at how few people left welfare for work. Certainly it is possible, even common, for AFDC recipients to escape welfare via earnings. But the vast majority of people who leave the welfare rolls are classified as leaving for other reasons. Although we cannot say why earnings exits account for such a modest portion of departures, the findings raise disturbing questions about the viability of reforms predicated on moving large numbers of people from welfare to work.

But this classification scheme does not provide a sense of the full importance of earnings in helping people escape welfare. Because the scheme is hierarchical and allows only one classification per exit, it is possible that significant earnings changes are more common than the 25 percent figure would suggest. A woman who marries *and* has substantial earnings in the year she leaves AFDC will be classified as having left via becoming a wife.

An alternative way to examine the possible role of earnings is to ask what fraction of all former welfare recipients had earnings in excess of some number—say, $6,000—in the first year they were off of welfare. Table 2.9 examines the possibility that women who became wives or who were classified as leaving welfare for other reasons had substantial earnings in their first year off of welfare. The table gives a somewhat more encouraging picture. We see in the last column that 41 percent of former welfare recipients earn over $6,000 in their first year off of the program, in constant 1992 dollars. Some 30 percent earn over $9,000—enough to push a family

Table 2.8 Percentage distribution of AFDC ending types

Ending type	Percentage of all endings
Female household head became a wife	29.4
No longer had eligible child	10.8
Head's earnings increased	25.0
Transfer income increased	12.1
Earnings of others increased	6.7
Family became smaller	5.4
Family moved	1.6
Unidentified	9.2
Total	100.0

Source: Authors' tabulation of the 21-year Panel Study of Income Dynamics.

of three above the poverty line. Many of these "high" earners were classified as having left for reasons other than earnings.[9]

Evidence from monthly data also calls into question our initial findings that earnings exits are only about one fourth of all exits. Monthly data allow one to pinpoint the reasons for exit more precisely. In annual data, we might observe that someone married in the year following her departure from welfare. We would classify this person as exiting because of marriage. But monthly data might show that the person left welfare in a month in which her earnings rose sharply, and didn't marry for many months later. A second feature of annual data is that it misses the shorter episodes off of welfare when someone may leave for work for a few months, then leave or lose her job, and return to welfare. Since these short-term episodes off of welfare may be disproportionately due to brief periods of employment, an annual approach may further understate the role of work, at least in brief exits.

Table 2.9   Percentage distribution of persons who have exited AFDC by
              earnings in first year after leaving welfare and by exit reason
              classification

Earnings in first year after AFDC receipt	Hierarchical exit classification				
	Female head became a wife	No longer had eligible child	Head's earnings increased	Other	Total
None	12.6	8.4	0.0	11.6	32.6
$1–$3,000	8.4	1.7	2.2	5.9	18.2
$3,001–$6,000	3.0	1.7	1.0	2.5	8.2
$6,001–$9,000	4.2	0.2	5.1	1.7	11.2
$9,001–$12,000	0.4	0.9	2.9	2.9	7.1
$12,001–$15,000	1.3	0.4	4.8	2.0	8.5
Over $15,000	4.5	1.1	4.9	3.8	14.3
Total[a]	34.4	14.4	20.9	30.4	100.0

Source: Authors' tabulation of the 21-year Panel Study of Income Dynamics.
a. These totals differ slightly from the numbers in Table 2.8 because persons with
missing earnings have been excluded. Figures may not sum exactly due to rounding.

Using monthly data from the Seattle/Denver Income Maintenance Experiments, Rebecca Blank (1986) found that 33 percent of
all completed welfare spells could be traced to an increase in earnings. R. M. Gritz and Thomas McCurdy (1991) estimated that for
young women in the National Longitudinal Survey of Youth, half
of all exits can be attributed to work. Gregory Weeks (1991) reports
that just over half of all welfare recipients who have left welfare
report on a survey that they left welfare to enter the labor market.
Using monthly data from the PSID from the 1984–1986 period,
Kathleen Harris (1992) classified 69 percent of exits as being work
related. And Pavetti's (1993) study of young mothers finds that 46
percent of young mothers leave welfare for work and just 11 percent
leave for marriage, remarriage, or reconciliation. Each of these stud-

ies uses somewhat different classification systems, but Pavetti is able to show that if she had used annual rather than monthly data, she would have classified 31 percent as earnings exits rather than the 45 percent she found using monthly data.

Thus the role of earnings in welfare exits depends on the time frame one examines and the way in which reasons are classified. Our initial classification scheme was almost certainly too narrow in its classifications. Nonetheless, to the extent that monthly earnings exits simply capture short-term episodes off of welfare, we wonder how significant work is in permanent or long-term exits from welfare. Research in this area is only beginning. If we had to pick a single number for the significance of work exits, we'd probably pick one closer to the 40 percent who had moderate earnings in their first year off welfare than the 25 percent we find using our hierarchical classification system.

What is clear from the evidence is that many welfare mothers do indeed leave welfare for work, though often they move quickly back to welfare. It is also clear, however, that the view that women who go on the welfare rolls are inevitably embroiled in dependence until their children get to be too old or until they marry is not supported by the facts. It makes sense to ask whether more welfare recipients could be assisted to increase their work and earnings and to leave welfare more quickly.

We can ask whether earnings exits are influenced by factors different from those that influence other exits. In other work and in models shown here, we have looked at the marginal factors that influence work versus other exits. Generally, the results are interesting, if unsurprising. Education and previous work experience are very powerful predictors of exiting with moderate earnings. These same factors have very little influence on other exit patterns. Thus women with good education and recent work experience are much more likely to leave welfare for work, but only slightly more likely to leave for marriage or other reasons. This result seems plausible, for one would expect work experience and education to be a greater influence on job prospects than on marriage prospects (though some economists might argue that they are related).

Conversely race and marital status have some influence on earnings exits, but they are much stronger in their influence on marriage and other exits. Never-married women are considerably less likely to leave for reasons other than work; they are slightly less likely to leave for work. Again, one wouldn't expect marital status to indicate as much about labor market outlook as on the odds the person will seek to marry or remarry. Holding all else equal, including marital status, African-Americans are somewhat less likely to leave welfare for work in a given period, and much less likely to leave welfare for marriage or other reasons.

Policy Dynamics

Information on dynamics has figured prominently in policy debates in recent years. Many credit such data with having a major influence on the Family Support Act and on President Clinton's discussion of a time-limited welfare system in which expectations for work would change dramatically after two years. Many important policy insights come from looking at dynamics. The first is the heterogeneity of the welfare caseload. The finding that most new recipients stay a relatively short time, but that long-term users account for a sizable majority of the caseload and of recipients, strongly highlights the overly simplistic stereotyping of both liberals and conservatives.

The heterogeneity apparent in the results also suggests that a targeting strategy could make sense. If we can identify the long-term recipients, and find a way to move them off of welfare quickly, we can realize sizable welfare savings. Such investments might thus make sense even if they are initially expensive. Information from this chapter and the work of many others can help us identify the potential long-term recipients.

Targeting Potentially Long-Term Recipients

Sensible targeting involves more than identifying long-term recipients. Decisions about targeting must also take into account the cost-effectiveness of the proposed intervention. Knowing someone is likely to be a long-term recipient is helpful only if an intervention can be found to shorten the stay or ameliorate any negative impacts.

Moreover, if the characteristic that serves as the basis of targeting is itself subject to change by the individual, critical incentive questions may arise. In addition, it may be deemed moral or politically unacceptable to target certain groups.

Nevertheless, there are important lessons here. It is abundantly clear that women with poor educational and work experience backgrounds generally fare poorly, regardless of their age and marital status. A good education and recent work experience are probably the two strongest indicators of earnings exits. Happily, one can easily imagine interventions that could focus on the problems of limited work experience and education. Yet even here, we must be wary of simplistic solutions. These recipients are often people who have failed in the traditional education system or the labor market. Returning them to the institutions in which they failed or that failed them may not be a sensible policy.

Never-married women also appear to warrant special attention. Indeed, if one were to select a single variable for targeting on the basis of predicted welfare duration, marital status probably would be the choice. Never-married women have especially long periods of dependence in the absence of intervention, and the group includes a sizable portion of new AFDC recipients (an estimated 43 percent). Still, one might worry about the signals that a program would send if it gave more services to mothers who had never married than to other mothers. And we have little information on whether there are particularly effective interventions for this group. Thus political, practical, and ethical problems may work against targeting on the basis of marital status. In this case, a program for young mothers, whether married or not, may be more appropriate.

The overall view we gain from these results is that, for three reasons, women with young children at the time they first receive AFDC may be very good candidates for targeted service interventions. First, the group is large. The overwhelming proportion (83 percent in Table 2.6) of all women beginning their first spell of AFDC have children under age six, and nearly two thirds have a child under age three.[10] Second, their expected future dependency is relatively great. And third, the presence of young children, per se, does not seem to be the cause of their especially long expected duration of welfare dependence. What we do not currently know is what causes the high probabilities of long-term dependence, nor do we have solid evidence on the effectiveness of alternative intervention strategies. We also do not yet have solid information on the degree to which the presence of young children complicates effective services delivery.[11] Nonetheless, these results make a compelling case for including mothers of preschool children in employment and training programs.

A related conclusion is that there is more reason than previously thought for targeting employment and training resources toward very young recipients of AFDC who are just beginning their dependency. These women have among the bleakest long-term prospects for achieving economic self-sufficiency. Furthermore, because of their youth, both they and their children may be more susceptible than others to any of the adverse effects of long-term welfare dependence. This reinforces the commonsense belief that teen mothers need special attention.

The evidence also suggests that some past targeting ideas may have been incorrect. The Work Incentive program, which preceded the Family Support Act, limited services to women with children over age five.[12] Women who entered AFDC when their children were very young often did not receive services at all. If we wait to serve recipients until their youngest child is over age five, we may have to wait five years, or more if there are subsequent births, before providing services. The earlier focus on women with no preschool-aged children reflected the view that programs were more likely to be effective in helping those with older children and the concern that mothers of young children should not be forced to work. Many women who might have been eager and able to achieve greater self-support, however, were left unserved.

The Family Support Act now requires the participation of mothers with children over three. This still leaves two thirds of mothers entering AFDC for the first time outside the program. States have the option of requiring participation when children are even younger.

Another questionable idea is to wait and serve only people who have been on welfare for a period of time. Many people, including ourselves in earlier work, have suggested the possible advantages of targeting some people at the beginning of their spell, but waiting several years before serving others. The idea has been that the short-term recipients move off quickly, and that by waiting one might serve a higher proportion of long-term recipients. The logic behind this prescription was that the chances of escaping welfare diminished rapidly after the first two years of a spell. Our more recent analyses suggest that taking a "wait-to-serve" approach may have fewer advantages than first presumed.

The problem with waiting before providing services is that in the meantime both the time that persons spend on welfare and the resources they consume are lost. If we wait and serve people who have been on welfare for two to four years, we have lost the opportunity to reduce welfare use in those first years of dependence. Certainly, we would be serving people with a greater chance of long-term welfare use, but the total welfare time *remaining* might not be particularly long.

Under a spell approach to measuring long-term dependency, the "wait-and-see" strategy seemed to make sense, because waiting was relatively effective at identifying potential long-term users, and the future welfare time in the spell of persons who had been on for more than two years was greater than the overall average time for those beginning welfare. When recidivism and lengths of repeat spells are considered, however, the conclusion is far less clear. First, it appears that persons with very short first spells of AFDC receipt may be more likely than average to return to AFDC. Failing to serve such persons may save initially, but because many return to welfare quickly their total time on welfare is eventually much greater than it appeared with a spell approach. Second, fewer persons have welfare duration of only a few years when recidivism is considered. Consequently, waiting for persons to experience a few years of total time on welfare before serving them screens out a relatively small portion of the recipient group in the long run.

Table 2.10 shows the effect of waiting to observe a period of dependency on target efficiency. It shows what happens if one waits for no years, two years, and four years before serving first-time AFDC recipients. By waiting for two years, one will serve about 63

Table 2.10　　Percentage of AFDC recipients at various stages of receipt
history, and average total and future durations of AFDC receipt

Stage of welfare receipt	Percentage of new recipients who reach spell stage (new beginnings)	Average number of years of AFDC receipt	Average number of years of future AFDC receipt
Just began	100.0	6.2	6.2
Exactly 2 years	63.4	8.9	6.9
Exactly 4 years	44.8	11.2	7.2

Source: Authors' tabulation of the 21-year Panel Study of Income Dynamics.

percent of all those who begin a first spell on AFDC. The expected total time on welfare for those served increases from 6.2 to 8.9 years. Thus one has improved the odds that one is serving potential long-term recipients who consume a disproportionate share of AFDC resources. Two years' worth of welfare have been lost in the meantime, however. The *future* time on welfare is only 6.9 years, just slightly higher than the 6.2 average for all those beginning AFDC.

The fiscal advantages from waiting to serve recipients appear to be quite modest. Although waiting does screen out some short-duration recipients, AFDC and Medicaid payments provided to recipients during the period they are served are lost, reducing possible welfare savings.

Monthly Dynamics, Cyclers, and the Role of Earnings

Some years back our initial work pointed out the highly dynamic nature of AFDC spells. Though long-term receipt got more attention than before, the predominant reaction we observed (in ourselves and others) was surprise at how dynamic welfare was. Later when we developed estimates of total time on welfare, reaction swung the other way: many were struck that when multiple spells were taken into account, welfare appeared to be long in many cases. And we tended to emphasize how rare earnings exits were.

Now, with additional information on monthly dynamics and alternative estimates of earnings exits, our views have partially swung back. There clearly is a remarkable amount of dynamics among welfare clients. The overwhelming proportion do leave a first spell, often very quickly. Often the departure is to work. But departures are all too often short lived. And cumulating over multiple spells, the total time is often great, even for cyclers.

The recognition that long-term welfare use often involves considerable cycling strongly suggests that single mothers may simply be unable to sustain self-support in an economic climate in which jobs pay too little, medical care is often not provided, and child-care costs are high. This finding points to a new direction for policy: making work genuinely feasible as an alternative to welfare. Policy should, perhaps, concentrate more on keeping people off welfare than on getting them off once. It may be relatively easy to get many people a low-paying job, but the job may not be sustainable as a source of economic provision.

Yet even monthly data show a disturbing group of people who seemingly never leave welfare. And they still are a large fraction of recipients at any point in time. Even Pavetti, who finds that 93 percent of new young recipients end their first spell within eight years of its beginning, still finds that the 7 percent who do not constitute nearly 40 percent of recipients at a point in time. Not every long-term recipient is a cycler, and without some form of intervention, many will stay on welfare for a very long time indeed.

From this examination of welfare dynamics we take four policy lessons:

- Recognize how dynamic and diverse the AFDC population is. Avoid simplistic stereotyping and the solutions they imply. One size cannot possibly fit all welfare recipients.

- Do target. Some people will have long spells otherwise, and they are where most of the dollars go. The poorly educated, those with little work experience, the never-married, and the young all deserve special attention.

- Don't wait. Waiting to see who becomes a long-term recipient mostly wastes time. And we find limited evidence that waiting until children reach a given age dramatically increases the ease of their mother's moving off welfare.

- Work as hard at keeping people off as one does at getting them off.

Observing these lessons alone does not mean that we will eliminate long-term welfare use. But ignoring them would probably prevent us from doing so.

3
Understanding Dependency

It is hard to miss the profound shift in emphasis and tone in poverty discussions over the past ten to fifteen years. A decade or two ago, the academic debate and to a large degree the popular debate were often focused on matters of adequacy, labor supply responses, tax rates, and opportunity. Now "dependency" is the current preoccupation.

The transformation of the debate is quite extraordinary, because it represents an implicit shift in behavioral models. In earlier debates, economists seemed to dominate with their emphasis on static choice models. Behavior could be understood by examining the choices people faced at any point in time. Changes in behavior could be induced by altering the available choices. Now the talk is often about lost confidence or distorted values that leave the poor with little sense of what their choices truly are and little desire to take control of their lives. Considerable debate remains, however, over whether welfare use and poverty are best understood by examining the choices people face or the values they possess.

The existence of long-term welfare use has led some to call for major new investments in people, some to call for the elimination of support, some to recommend workfare, and still others to emphasize nonwelfare alternative sources of support. Which of these options is most appropriate depends heavily on the causes and nature of dependency.

The term *dependency* is used quite loosely in public discussion and in most academic work. It is sometimes nothing more than a synonym for long-term welfare use. But dependency is commonly applied to situations in which people who could conceivably provide for themselves fail to do so, and as a result it often has a pejorative connotation. Those who are dependent are inactive, ineffectual, and even irresponsible in the eyes of many. Most popular presentations of the subject move quickly into questions of motivation, expectations, and the "culture of poverty."

Both the popular and the academic treatments of dependency have, in general, been flawed by incomplete, inconsistent, or nonexistent behavioral models. In many works, such as those providing empirical estimates of how long welfare lasts, the lack of a behavioral model does not cloud the validity of the results. In principle, the duration of welfare is a relatively objective measurement. Yet even in these cases, the interpretation of the results, particularly for policy purposes, can be quite different depending on the behavioral basis for the findings.

After an extensive review of the literature, we find three types of models that offer influential explanations for dependency: rational choice models, expectancy models, and class cultural models. Each emphasizes different factors and a different conception of behavior. In simple terms, they emphasize, respectively, choices and incentives, confidence and control, and values and culture. Each model makes somewhat different empirical predictions about how dependency works.

How are we to decide which models of dependency are most appropriate? Obviously we need to find areas where each makes different predictions about empirically observable relationships and then compare the predictions with research results. Models can be fruitfully contrasted by comparing their predictions to the empirical findings in four areas: (1) static work, welfare, and poverty patterns, (2) the duration and dynamics of welfare, (3) policy influences on work and welfare, and (4) family structure patterns and correlates.

Models of Dependency

Rational Choice Models

The dominant paradigm in economics and policy analysis is the rational choice model. Rational choice models suggest that individuals examine the options they face, evaluate them according to their tastes and preferences, and then select the option that brings them the greatest utility or satisfaction. To understand behavior, both choices and preferences must be understood. But in actual practice, the emphasis in rational choice models is on understanding the choices people face and the ways in which these change.

According to such models, long-term welfare use should be seen as a series of reasoned choices in the light of available options. Naturally both the characteristics of the welfare system and the nature of outside opportunities will influence such use.

One of the most striking ironies in the current debate is that the term "dependency" has almost no currency in a rational choice framework. Many who worry about dependency speak of perverse values and irresponsible behavior, or of how the inhumane structure of the welfare system robs people of their dignity and self-esteem, reducing their ability and willingness to gain control over their own lives. Dependency thus implies either a change in values (preferences) as people acquire the "welfare habit" and/or limited motivation in the first place. Traditional choice theories do not consider either possibility.

The reticence to judge preferences or to treat them as endogenous seems to be both pragmatically and ethically based. Models in which preferences are changeable are likely to be quite complex, especially if the individual is assumed to recognize that current behavior can affect future preferences. Moreover, any decision that one set of preferences is more legitimate than others moves such models into a very different realm, where what constitutes a "rational choice" becomes subjective and ambiguous. To judge the choices of others smacks of paternalism and elitism.

Rational choice models emphasize the decisions individuals make about whether and how to use welfare. Consider for example a healthy, single mother with two children whose father is absent. Assume that like 63 percent of female heads of families, she receives no child support or alimony (U.S. House, Ways and Means 1992). She has two potential sources of support: her own earnings and government assistance. The key question is whether she will rely heavily on welfare or support herself and her family through other means.

The Committee on Ways and Means provides a table showing what the options would look like if she lived in Pennsylvania in January 1991. Table 3.1 shows that a woman earning $10,000 per year (roughly $5.00 per hour) is only slightly better off than one who does not work at all. Her disposable income will have risen about $2,000, she will have day-care and other work expenses, and she will have lost her Medicaid protection.[1] Even if she finds a job paying $15,000 per year ($7.50 per hour), her disposable income will be only about $2,600 higher than that of a woman who does no work and collects welfare.

From the rational choice perspective, Table 3.1 suggests rather strongly that under current law work often makes little financial sense unless: (1) the woman works full-time, (2) she commands a wage well above the minimum, (3) day-care costs are low, and (4) available welfare benefits are low. In general one would expect these conditions to be true for women who are well educated, have previous work experience, have older children, have relatively few children (since the number of children affects both benefits and day-care costs), and live in low-benefit states. The rational choice model predicts that these factors ought to play a major role in determining the level of work.

With no facts other than these, what would we expect under the choice paradigm about poverty and welfare use? First, given the lack of additional sources of financial support, we would anticipate much higher incidence of poverty among single-parent families than among two-parent ones. Moreover, either we would expect women to work full-time at moderately paying jobs that put them off of welfare or we would expect to see them on welfare. One would anticipate that many single parents would choose welfare over work, especially in light of the small gains from working shown in Table 3.1. The ones for whom work could make sense are those with high pay, low day-care costs, and low potential welfare benefits. Nor would we expect to see many people mixing work and welfare simultaneously.

One of the more interesting and striking results of the choice model is that absent opportunities to leave welfare through marriage or other nonemployment routes, people ought to stay on welfare a long time. The model suggests that it is hard to earn one's way off of welfare. Moreover, the circumstances that make work a difficult and often quite unattractive choice change slowly.

Thus the choice model predicts that earnings exits will be rare, that earnings exits will be closely related to factors influencing the relative attractiveness of work, and that people who do not find nonearnings ways off of welfare will stay on welfare a long time. If the welfare population were highly dynamic due to earnings exits, and if many people stayed on for a few years and then earned their way off of it, choice models would be quite suspect. One would also expect to see some response to changed incentives. If welfare benefits fell or economic conditions improved, one would expect to see fewer people on welfare and more people working.

A choice model can also be applied to the marriage, remarriage, separation, divorce, and out-of-wedlock childbearing decisions that lead to the creation or elimination of single-parent households in the first place. The two major events that create a single-parent family are divorce or separation in a two-parent family with children, and the birth of a child to an unmarried mother. What are the options and incentives that might influence such decisions?

There is a literature on the economics of marriage and divorce, pioneered by Gary Becker (1973, 1981). This work often emphasizes the potential gains to marriage created by "joint production," specialization (with one person in home activities, the other in market activities), and returns to scale (arising out of the fact that a person can live more cheaply as part of a couple than alone). Generally such models suggest that any increased earning potential of men will improve the appeal of marriage, that any increased earning potential of women may diminish it, and that any increased potential of nonwage income outside of marriage (such as welfare) will diminish the appeal of marriage. Other factors, such as love and responsibility, are obviously involved in these choices. Nonetheless, most observers seem to agree at least that higher male earnings ought to improve marriage prospects and that higher welfare might increase divorce and out-of-wedlock births.

The predictions of the choice model can be summarized as follows.

Table 3.1 Earnings and benefits for a mother with two children with day-care expenses, after four months on job (January 1991, in Pennsylvania)

Earnings	EITC[a]	AFDC[b]	Food stamps[c]	Medicaid	Taxes			Work expenses[e]	Disposable income
					Social Security	Federal income[d]	State income		
0	0	$5,052	$2,166	Yes	0	0	0	0	$7,218[f]
$2,000	$346	4,892	1,854	Yes	$153	0	0	$600	8,339[f]
4,000	692	3,292	1,974	Yes	306	0	0	1,200	8,452[f]
5,000	865	2,492	2,034	Yes	383	0	0	1,500	8,508[f]
6,000	1,038	1,692	2,094	Yes	459	0	0	1,800	8,565[f]
7,000	1,211	892	2,154	Yes	536	0	0	2,100	8,621[f]
8,000	1,235	0	2,241	Yes[g]	612	0	0	2,400	8,464[f]
9,000	1,235	0	2,061	Yes[h]	689	0	$38	2,700	8,869[f]
10,000	1,235	0	1,881	No[h]	765	0	210	3,000	9,141[f]
15,000	772	0	0	No[i]	1,148	0	315	4,200	10,019
20,000	154	0	0	No	1,530	$283	420	5,200	12,721
30,000	0	0	0	No	2,295	1,943	630	5,400	19,732
50,000	0	0	0	No	3,825	6,405	1,050	5,400	33,320

Source: U.S. House, Ways and Means (1991).

a. Assumes that both children are over age one. If one were younger, the Earned Income Tax Credit (EITC) would be larger (maximum of $1,592 at earnings of $8,000–$10,000).

b. Assumes these deductions: $120 monthly standard allowance (which would drop to $90 after one year on the job) and child-care costs equal to 20 percent of earnings, up to maximum of $350 for two children.

c. Assumes these deductions: 20 percent of earnings, $122 monthly standard deduction, and child-care costs equal to 20 percent of wages, up to maximum of $320 for two children.

d. Head of household rates in effect for 1992. The dependent care tax credit reduces tax liability at earnings of $15,000 and above.

e. Assumed to equal 10 percent of earnings up to maximum of $100 monthly, plus child-care costs equal to 20 percent of earnings up to the maximum allowed for AFDC ($350 for two children).

f. In addition, the benefits from Medicaid could be added, but are not. In Pennsylvania, the cost of Medicaid for a three-person AFDC family averaged about $2,304 in fiscal year 1989.

g. Family would qualify for Medicaid because the mother, by law, would be deemed still an AFDC recipient, even though no AFDC would be paid; her calculated benefit would be below the minimum amount ($10 monthly) payable.

h. Family would qualify for Medicaid for twelve months after leaving AFDC under the 1988 Family Support Act. State must offer Medicaid to all children up to age six whose family income is not above 133 percent of the federal poverty guideline (ceiling of $14,850 for a family of three in 1991) and to children over age six born after September 1, 1983 (up to age 7 1/3 in January 1991), whose family income is below the poverty guideline ($11,140 for a family of three).

i. After losing her Medicaid transitional benefits, to regain eligibility, mother must spend down on medical expenses to the state's medically needy income limit ($5,400 in September 1989).

Static work, welfare, and poverty patterns—Poverty, work, and welfare should be tied to socioeconomic variables such as education, age and number of children, and work experience. We expect to see little mixing of work and welfare, because there is no real benefit in doing so. Generally one would expect part-time work to be less common among single parents than among wives.

Welfare duration and dynamics—Earnings exits ought to be relatively rare, especially for women with low potential wages or moderate welfare benefits. One would expect close links between economic factors and the earnings exits observed. Marriage exits ought to be linked to choices people have for partners. The choice model is not sophisticated enough to make very precise predictions about the frequency of such exits, but marriage would be expected to account for much of the dynamics, since earnings exits look so difficult. The model also suggests that the difficulty of leaving welfare ought not to vary much with time on the program.

Policy influences on work and welfare—Choice models emphasize incentives in the transfer system as the primary policy lever that might be used to change behavior. They also suggest that training and other programs to raise the potential wages of welfare recipients would be helpful. They offer little insight into questions of mandatory versus voluntary participation, though choice models are traditionally espoused by those who favor individual choice over compulsion.

Patterns of family structure changes—Predictions are not clear-cut, because it is difficult to observe all the dimensions of choices that ought to influence family structure decisions. The model does suggest that higher welfare benefits ought to have some influence on divorce, separation, and births to unmarried women. The financial position of men can be expected to have an important influence. Earnings and work by women have an ambiguous effect, but most theorists posit that on balance employment will increase the potential independence of women enough to lead to fewer intact families.

Expectancy Models

Expectancy models emphasize the individual's sense of control over a desired outcome. People will act in a certain way only if they have an "expectancy" that the action is likely to move them toward a desired result (Atkinson 1964; Gurin and Gurin 1970).

Expectancy theories typically posit a two-way relationship between confidence and sense of control, on the one hand, and the outcomes people actually experience, on the other. People who succeed gain confidence. Those who fail lose confidence. Persons suffering repeated failure may lose "motivation."

According to expectancy theories, dependency may result when people lose a sense of control over their lives—when they cease to believe that they can realistically get off of welfare. People become overwhelmed by their situation and lose the ability to seek out and use the opportunities available.

A related notion is that dependency may reflect a lack of information. In expectancy models, people often incorrectly perceive their level of control over their destiny. Such misperception would be quite likely if people simply did not have important information. A young woman who does not understand or who has not thought seriously about birth control could understandably see pregnancy as something outside her control.

Such theories come much closer than the rational choice paradigm to capturing popular notions of dependency. They rarely offer a very systematic sense of what constitutes control and failure, however. Exactly what constitutes a loss of control in the welfare setting is quite difficult to determine. For example, would eliminating welfare give people a lesser or a greater sense of control over their destiny? Moreover, since such theories often posit that actual lack of control and the perceived lack of control are interrelated, it can be very difficult to infer whether people are objectively without power or whether they only perceive themselves to be.

The expectancy models require thinking about much more than current choices. Past successes and failures as well as current perceptions are critical in models that emphasize confidence, control, and information. It makes less sense to model just one set of behavior (such as long-term welfare use) independent of the events that led the person to welfare in the first place. The picture of dependency is more encompassing and comprehensive than that provided by choice theory, but inevitably the models are less well defined and harder to test.

Dependency might arise in several ways according to the expectancy model. A married couple might divorce or separate for any of a myriad of reasons. Expectancy models emphasize that the divorce itself may have profound effects on the woman and on her ability to cope with her environment. How she feels about herself, how she perceives the world, and how she fares in her new situation will critically influence her behavior.

If the woman enters the welfare system, she encounters additional forces that tend to diminish her sense of control and self-esteem. The system pries into her private life. Administrators want to know her income and assets. They want to know where the father of her child is. The newly single parent may be asked to return for numerous appointments, to return with new documentation such as rent checks or earnings statements. She may be required to register for a variety of programs supposedly designed to help her, but which often seem more concerned with ensuring that she obeys rules.

The system may even seem designed to thwart the efforts of those who seek to escape through work. If the woman finds part-time work, she not only gets no net increase in income (as the choice model emphasizes), but she is identified as an "error-prone case" and is asked for even more documentation to be certain that she is not cheating. If she does get off of the system, she quickly loses her medical benefits. This loss may be important, not only because there is some financial value associated with such coverage (the choice model would consider this), but also because of the psychological effect it might have in making women fear that by working they are facing even more uncertainty and are putting their children at medical risk.

Some women might react with anger and frustration to such a system and seek to leave it as quickly as possible. In common with the choice model, this model might suggest that those in the best position to leave would do so. Others might try to gain control of their lives by "gaming" the system, doing the minimum necessary to keep the checks coming. But many may lose even more confidence and feel more isolated from the rest of society. The longer one stays in the system, the harder it becomes to break out.

The situation might be even more difficult for an unmarried

woman. If the woman lives in a ghetto, there is even more tragedy and deprivation to contend with, according to advocates of this model. She may have done poorly in school. The young men around her are often unemployed. Crime and drugs may heighten her sense of physical insecurity. She may become sexually active with little thought of the consequences. Or she may knowingly allow herself to become pregnant. Either way she may decide to keep the child and enter the welfare system. To a girl with little chance of escaping or controlling her rather hostile environment, having a baby may seem one of the few ways of gaining some control and significance. But once pregnant, she may feel frightened and helpless. When the child arrives, there are new stresses and struggles. And once in the welfare system, the young mother's sense of failure is heightened.

Although very different in tone and emphasis from the choice model, the expectancy model can be difficult to distinguish empirically. Confidence and control are in part based on the outcomes of past experiences. Those who actually have fewer and poorer choices may well have failed more often in the past and thus perform worse now. A dropout may do poorly in the labor market because the choices are limited or because she lacks confidence and information. Still, there are several dimensions on which somewhat different predictions might be based:

Static work, welfare, and poverty patterns—Because the expectancy model is one in which life history and expectations are particularly important, it is difficult to use it to make predictions about who will be poor or on welfare at a point in time. Like the choice-based story, it would suggest that those with better educational and work experience would do better. This model holds that marital status would predict work and welfare status, whereas a choice-based model would not. Moreover, it suggests that people's sense of confidence and control influences life events.

Welfare duration and dynamics—In this domain, the choice and expectancy models yield sharply different predictions. If people's ability to leave welfare is more a matter of their sense of control and self-esteem than of the choices immediately available, then a far more dynamic welfare system is predicted. Some people will enter the system in a time of crisis and stress and after a period regain control and start a better life. If confidence and information is the limiting factor rather than choices, then earnings exits ought to be more common, especially in early years. Noneconomic variables such as marital status and sense of control ought to affect welfare durations generally and earnings exits in particular. Perhaps most important, the longer one stays on welfare, the harder it ought to be to get off.

Policy influences on work and welfare—In these models the human side of the welfare program may be far more important than its financial incentives. To help people move off of welfare, policies that emphasize giving increased confidence and control would be most helpful. Support systems like day care, medical protection, sources of personal reinforcement, and information services all ought to play significant roles.

Patterns of family structure changes—Perceptions of limited control, isolation, lack of confidence, and evidence of past failures would be linked to out-of-wedlock births. Information about birth control ought to exert an influence. It seems harder to say what should influence divorce. Women with a greater sense of control may be happier in their marriages, but they may also be more inclined to leave if things become desperate. There are few sharp predictions from this model about what variables would influence family patterns nationally.

Cultural Models

Our last category is a rather uneasy collection of theories that typically emphasize that groups differ widely in values, orientations, and expectations.[2] Probably the most well known theories are those presented in the "culture of poverty" and "underclass" literature. According to culture of poverty characterizations, those trapped by such a culture are said to exhibit antisocial and counterproductive behavior. According to Ken Auletta, the underclass is a group that "feels excluded from society, rejects commonly accepted values, suffers from *behavioral* as well as *income* deficiencies. They don't just tend to be poor; to most Americans their behavior seems aberrant" (Auletta 1982, p. xiii; emphasis in the original).

No one contests that culture critically influences behavior. What distinguishes the cultural literature on dependency is its claim that values, attitudes, and expectations of certain subgroups are well outside the mainstream. Models that emphasize norms and mores assume that adverse values will develop and persist among groups of people who are said to be isolated geographically and socially from the rest of society. These people live in geographic areas of concentrated deprivation where an "underclass" can be maintained.

Conservative treatments of cultural theories acknowledge that people in ghettos live in a state of severe disadvantage. Schools are not very effective. The jobs that ghetto residents tend to be qualified for pay poorly and don't offer a promising future. Mainstream routes to success do not appear very available or attractive. At the same time, there are several obvious means of support that allow one to avoid striving for traditional success, such as drugs, violence, or theft. One can also turn to the government for aid. Not surprisingly, a large number of people choose one of these options.

So far this conception has much in common with the choice model. It differs from the choice model in postulating that with so many people adopting nontraditional modes of behavior, the society's mores begin to change. Living in a world where the most visible successes are criminals and where government benefits seem to come most to those who have eschewed traditional work or family patterns, people begin to change their attitudes and mores. The person who works long hours at low pay seems to be a chump. Those who can game the system become heroes. The community increasingly comes to condone such behavior. Welfare seems like a natural and legitimate alternative to either marriage or work. Men often feel little responsibility to support a family.

The more liberal version of the cultural model, such as that offered by William Julius Wilson (1985, 1987; Wilson and Neckerman 1986), describes similar outcomes but a different diagnosis. A significant drop in employment opportunities owing to the changing industrial mix and the outmigration of jobs from the city makes traditional market opportunities scarce in the inner city. Simultaneously, the outmigration of black professionals has left a community that consists mainly of people with weak links to mainstream success. Gone are many of the role models and community leaders that emerged in a day when the minority community was more integrated economically. Moreover, as those with reasonably good jobs have left the ghetto, they also have taken with them the critical inside connections that help young people into the labor market. What is left is a community with few examples of mainstream success. Young men have no jobs. Many are in jail. They make very unattractive marriage partners, and thus intact families do not form. Welfare and criminal activity help to sustain the community. People lose sight of and lose the capacity to pursue mainstream options. They become an "underclass."

Liberal cultural theories emphasize the loss of jobs and the restraints on mobility of low-income minority residents; the conservative scenario worries about welfare and government benefits. But some elements are common to both. In both scenarios dependency is related to concentration and isolation. Adverse values arise when disadvantaged and relatively unsuccessful people live together with little contact with the rest of the society. It is only in areas of high poverty that these models really make sense.

A second feature, which is perhaps more prominent in the conservative version, is that poverty and welfare use have a heavy intergenerational component. Families with distorted values, or children raised in homes where welfare is a primary source of income, find welfare, out-of-wedlock births, and lack of work a normal and largely acceptable fact of life. As a result a negative pattern in one generation is passed to the next. In addition, the versions of the cultural models that emphasize values as being a major problem suggest that values among the dependent poor are truly different from those of middle-class Americans.

In a ghetto setting, the cultural and expectancy models share much in common. Wilson's treatment seems to draw heavily on expectancy models. In most cultural models, however, the emphasis is very different. The expectancy models emphasize lack of control and hopelessness. The cultural models suggest that what is lacking are the social norms that condemn criminal activity, violence, and births out of wedlock. Welfare is viewed as a right and reasonable way to support oneself. What are the testable empirical predictions of cultural models?

Static work, welfare, and poverty patterns—The cultural model is distinguished most sharply by its emphasis on concentration. Those raised in bad neighborhoods are expected to fare poorly socially and economically. Cultural models also imply that children raised in poverty or dependence are likely to be similarly situated as adults. And most cultural models imply that those in ghettos and similar subgroups will likely have antisocial or otherwise adverse values and attitudes.

Welfare duration and dynamics—For those in ghetto communities, cultural models suggest a stagnant welfare population. Long-term welfare use should be related to concentrated poverty, previous family dependence, and adverse attitudes. The model implicitly predicts that welfare will be more dynamic for those who are not in ghettos. Because choices, incentives, confidence, and information are not the major problems causing dependency, those with reasonable values and expectations can gain independence.

Policy influences on work and welfare—Predictions about the impact of policy choices differ dramatically depending on what the origins of the problems in the ghetto seem to be. The liberal view emphasizes the importance of the economy and jobs. Conservatives emphasize the importance of disincentives in the welfare system.

Patterns of family structure changes—Concentration, family history, and attitudes ought to predict family structure behavior. Conservative versions of the model usually emphasize that incentives in the welfare system may be playing a larger role than they should because people are not sufficiently concerned about having children out of wedlock.

Comparing the Findings with the Predictions

The predictions of the various models are summarized in Table 3.2. A quick look reveals that there are some important differences in the predictions of various models. There is a great deal of evidence that might bear directly or indirectly on these issues. A selective

Table 3.2 Different predictions of choice, expectancy, and cultural models

Predictions on	Choice models	Expectancy models	Cultural models
Static work, welfare, and poverty patterns	Closely linked to factors influencing potential earnings Mixing work and welfare uncommon	Noneconomic factors such as marital status also important Perceived control critical	Concentrated deprivation and neighborhood characteristics closely linked to poverty and welfa Intergenerational transmission of poverty and welfare Attitudes and values different among the poor especially in areas of concentrated poverty
Welfare duration and dynamics	Earnings exits rare Earnings exits tied to economic variables Difficulty of leaving welfare changes little with time on program	Welfare relatively dynamic with earnings exits more common Earnings exits also linked to noneconomic variables such as marital status and perceived control Welfare can "trap," making it harder to leave as time in the program increases	Welfare short-live for those with positive attitudes Welfare durations linked to neighborhood characteristics

Table 3.2 (continued)

Predictions on	Choice models	Expectancy models	Cultural models
Policy influences on work and welfare	Benefit levels and other incentives are critical Training or other methods to raise potential earnings helpful	Human side of welfare more important than incentives Policies that increase confidence and control most helpful Supplemental supports such as day care and medical care more important than pure financial benefit in helping people leave welfare	Greater obligations and expectations are important More choices and control are important
Family structure patterns and correlates	Economic variables such as welfare benefits, earnings of men, and earnings of women important	Confidence, perception of control, evidence of past failure influence births to unmarried women Less clear predictions on divorce and separation patterns	Attitudes and neighborhood attributes critical Family history in welfare important

review of the key findings with the most immediate relevance follows.

Static Work, Welfare, and Poverty Patterns

The three models give different predictions about the pattern of work and welfare that should be observed at a moment in time. Choice theory suggests that women with high net earning potential ought to be far more likely to work than women with low potential earnings. Welfare participation ought to be closely linked to economic variables. Expectancy models emphasize that direct measures of control, confidence, and expectations are important. Indirect measures such as high school record, work experience, and fertility history may be indications of past success and failure and thus influence people's perceptions and abilities to control their lives. The cultural models emphasize a close link between poverty and welfare use. They tend to predict a high level of the intergenerational transmission of poverty. What does the evidence actually show?

Participation patterns in AFDC. Evidence about participation offers substantial, though only partial, confirmation of the predictions of choice theory. Every significant study of welfare participation has shown that economic variables are strong predictors of who is working fully and who is on welfare. After reviewing a number of studies of participation, Robert Moffitt (1992) concluded that participation in AFDC is positively affected by the level of benefits, and that potential earnings and unearned income have strong negative effects on participation.

As the choice models predict, education, number of children, unemployment rates, and work experience all have an important influence on participation. Of course, some of these influences could be interpreted using the expectancy or culture theories as effects of confidence or ambition.

Much of the evidence about work is consistent with a choice-based model of work and welfare behavior. Under the current rules, choice models predict that single parents ought either to work all the time or to be on welfare and not working at all. In March 1992 roughly half of all single mothers worked full-time (about the same percentage as married mothers), and only 11 percent worked part-time (as opposed to 18 percent of married mothers).[3] Ellwood (1988) shows that the women who do work are much more likely to be high school graduates, more likely to have work experience, and less likely to have young children. Those who work full-time typically report wages in excess of $5 per hour.

The choice model also suggests that those on welfare would rarely work during the time they were collecting benefits. The evidence supports this prediction as well. Program data from 1990 show that only 8 percent of women on welfare were working at all (U.S. House, Ways and Means 1992, p. 676). Even before the 1981 changes in work incentives, only 14 percent to 18 percent of recipients were working in any year between 1968 and 1980 (Moffitt 1992).[4]

But the choice models cannot explain all of the evidence so easily. Work and welfare patterns also seem to be strongly related to marital status. On average, never-married mothers work far less than divorced mothers. Half of the divorced mothers with children under six worked full-time in March 1986, while only a quarter of those who were never married did. A significant part of this difference can be explained by other factors such as education and work experience, but a sizable marital status effect seems to remain even after controlling for other observed characteristics. Marital status may be capturing some unmeasured abilities, but its strength as a predictor seems most consistent with lack of confidence and control or adverse values playing some role.

Moreover, even though economic and incentive factors can explain a lot of the cross-sectional variation in welfare participation, they do not seem to be able to account for an important part of the variations in welfare participation over time. In the late 1960s and early 1970s, there was a sizable increase in the fraction of single parents who began receiving AFDC. Only a few studies, such as Moffitt (1986b) and Michel (1980), have been done, and the models used have been relatively simplistic.

These studies show that some of the increases in program participation may have been a result of both a reduction in the stigma of AFDC receipt and legislative changes that eliminated residency requirements and the man-in-the-house rule (Moffitt 1992). Changing noneconomic rules, of course, is an alteration of available choices, but not of the sort usually captured in choice models. But altered attitudes are inconsistent with the model of choice where preferences are assumed to be fixed.

In fact, economists have not been particularly successful in explaining the remarkable growth in labor force participation of all women (married and unmarried) since the 1960s. Women appear to be influenced by many factors outside the traditional economic choice models. Even though long-term dependency is both logical and predictable based on such a model, social norms and expectations clearly play a major role in work decisions. Note, however, that while this means that values seem to matter, it provides no direct evidence that welfare use is associated with deviant values.

A significant portion of the variation in the caseload does seem to be related to more traditional economic factors. During the 1970s and 1980s, real benefits fell and the caseload as a fraction of all single parents fell as well. These changes do not seem to have been analyzed in detail, but they appear to be consistent with trends in benefit levels and other program parameters that have left more women ineligible.

The relationship between perceived control and achievement. A strong prediction of expectancy models is that people who perceive they have less control will fare worse than people who are more confident even if they face the same opportunities. This is a difficult concept to test, because one needs to find people with the same "objective" opportunity and then look to see if differing perceptions matter.

There is evidence that people who have less sense of control are less successful and are at greater risk of poverty. Martha Hill et al. (1985) and Paul Andrisani (1978) report that various measures of personal efficacy and control are correlated with income in the predicted fashion. A greater fear of failure is associated with lower earnings. June O'Neill et al. (1984) found a weak association between measures of personal efficacy and welfare durations. Leonard

Goodwin (1983, p. 129) also concluded that "high or low expectations to achieve economic independence lead to high or low levels of achieved independence." Nancy Goodban (1985) reports that almost 60 percent of teenage mothers in New Haven, Connecticut, felt that the reasons they were on welfare were beyond their control.

As Hill et al. and many others have pointed out, it is very difficult to determine cause and effect. People who are less successful and who have failed more often probably *do* have less control over their lives and are at greater risk of failing. Hill and her colleagues note that involuntary changes in life such as a job loss or a forced move are associated with a later fall in measures of personal efficacy. The authors concluded that motivation and confidence were more the result than the cause of success or failure. Goodwin (1983) reached the similar conclusion that expectations of economic independence are strongly affected by the experience of success or failure in the work world.

Mary Corcoran and her colleagues (1985) state, "There is virtually no consistent evidence that motivational and psychological characteristics measured in the study affect subsequent achievement, either within or across generations." Andrisani (1981) claims to have found the opposite, though his findings are sharply disputed by Greg Duncan and James Morgan (1981). The literature is inconclusive at best. The evidence seems to lean toward an almost nihilistic judgment that motivation has no impact on success.

There is, however, something odd about a literature that seems to suggest that behavior and outcomes influence confidence and even motivation, but that confidence and motivation have few important effects on behavior. The notion that effort, motivation, and confidence influence success appears to be one of the strongest norms in American life. What the evidence more likely indicates is that confidence, control, and motivation are hard to measure.

Direct evidence on attitudes of welfare recipients. Cultural models talk about motivation to some degree, and they emphasize values about work and welfare. There are not very many widely cited studies that have looked at attitudes toward work and welfare, as opposed to people's personal sense of efficacy. Studies in the early 1970s (such as Goodwin [1972] and Kaplan and Tausky [1972]) showed a strong reported work ethic on the part of welfare recipients. In a more recent book, Goodwin reported that "acceptance or rejection of the idea of welfare or work has no effect on the achievement of economic independence by welfare recipients judged able to work. There is virtually no evidence that welfare dependency is caused by preference for welfare" (Goodwin 1983, p. 129).

Others, notably Lawrence Mead (1986), assert that evidence such as Goodwin's merely shows that the poor would like to work as long as the conditions are right. Mead claims, rather, that evidence seems to indicate that "work is normative for the poor, but is not something they feel they *must* do, whatever the personal cost. . . . To use Lon Fuller's distinction, the work ethic for the disadvantaged appears to represent 'a morality of aspiration' but not of 'duty'" (Mead 1986, p. 81).

In our estimation, this is a debate and a literature that has not been particularly productive. No matter what the results of surveys are, opponents seem ready to assert that they reflect measurement error or false reporting. Almost anyone will work if the job is right. And there are jobs that almost anyone would refuse to do. Judging whether the poor are really willing to take the jobs that others think they ought to seems to hinge far more on political and moral philosophy than on well-defined concepts of what constitutes an acceptable and appropriate attachment to the labor force.

Evidence on the concentration of poverty. Virtually all theories classified here as cultural emphasize concentration of poverty in explaining the existence and persistence of poverty and dependence. These models clearly suggest that neighborhoods, especially very bad neighborhoods, ought to play an important role in the life chances of young people. There are two logical questions: what fraction of poverty and welfare use can be found in concentrated poverty areas, and what links have been established between neighborhood characteristics and later outcomes?

Most of the work to date has dealt with poverty and work patterns overall rather than welfare use specifically. A wide range of authors have used data from the census to determine the proportion of all poor persons who are found in high-poverty neighborhoods. To the surprise of many, the studies almost universally conclude that the majority of poverty is not ghetto poverty. Most discussions of concentrated ghettos focus on big city, high-poverty neighborhoods. Table 3.3 shows what proportion of the nation's poor population can be found in high-poverty census tracts in metropolitan areas.

The table indicates that just 12 percent of the poor and 26 percent of the black poor are found in neighborhoods with census tract poverty rates of 40 percent or more. Most of the literature reaches similar conclusions. A somewhat different analysis has been done by Errol Ricketts and Isabel Sawhill (1986). They looked at the number of people (poor and nonpoor in all cities) who lived in census tracts where there was a high degree of behavioral troubles as measured by dropout levels, prime-age males not in the labor force, welfare recipients, and female household heads. They conclude that "in 1980, using our definition of underclass areas, there were 2.6 million people . . . living in such areas. Not all of these people are poor, nor do all of them engage in underclass behaviors, but they all live in neighborhoods where such behaviors are common" (Ricketts and Sawhill 1986, p. 7).

There is little information on welfare use by neighborhood pov-

Table 3.3   Distribution of poor persons by residence characteristics, 1990 (in thousands)

Race	United States		Metropolitan areas[a]		Ghetto areas[b]	
All	31,743	100.0%	22,833	71.9%	3,938	12.4%
Black	8,441	100.0	6,660	78.9	2,196	26.0
Hispanic	5,403	100.0	4,756	88.0	1,030	19.1
Non-Hispanic white[c]	17,899	100.0	11,417	63.8	712	4.0

Source: Unpublished calculations by Paul A. Jargowsky based on tract-level 1990 Census data.

a. Adjustments have been made to metropolitan-area boundaries to improve comparability with 1980 data. See Jargowsky (forthcoming).

b. Ghetto areas are defined as metropolitan census tracts with overall poverty rates of 40 percent or higher.

c. Estimated, because of limitations in the tract level data. Although Hispanics can be either white or black, the vast majority of Hispanics identify themselves as either white or "other race." Thus subtracting the black and Hispanic figures from the total yields a residual that is a good estimate for non-Hispanic white and other races.

erty level, but one can infer from published materials that in 1980, fewer than 8 percent of persons reporting public assistance income were in the very high poverty areas in large cities (U.S. Census 1985b, table 1; 1984, table 307). Thus evidence does not support a view that concentrated urban poverty is implicated in anything more than a small minority of observed welfare or poverty cases. Its role could be considerably larger in the very severe poverty and dependency cases, however.

There seem to be no studies that break down either welfare recipients, the *long-term* poor, or *long-term* welfare recipients (as opposed to all poor persons) by neighborhood poverty rate. Part of the problem is that the links between neighborhood data and longitudinal data necessary to make such determinations have not been available. Still, since the long-term recipient represents a large proportion of the poor at any point in time (see Chapter 2), it is unlikely that the results for the persistently poor would be dramatically different from the results for all the poor.

The second question is whether neighborhood conditions influence children's success. For the minority of poor persons in high-poverty areas, how serious are the negative neighborhood effects? There is considerable evidence that in very high poverty areas, neighborhood conditions are quite adverse. Existing studies seem to support Wilson's conclusion that the "communities of the underclass are plagued by massive joblessness, flagrant and open lawlessness, [and] low achieving schools" (Wilson 1987, p. 58). But the question that remains is just how influential the factors are.

Christopher Jencks and Susan Mayer (1990) offer an excellent review of the existing literature on school and neighborhood effects. They conclude that the research to date does not support firm conclusions. They offer two tentative hypotheses:

- When neighbors set social standards for one another or create institutions that serve an entire neighborhood, affluent neighbors are likely to be an advantage.

- When neighbors compete with one another for a scarce resource, such as social standing, high school grades, or teenage jobs, affluent neighbors are likely to be a disadvantage.

Because the balance between these two kinds of influence varies from one outcome to another, there is no general rule dictating that affluent neighbors will always be an advantage or a disadvantage.

Jencks and Mayer offer the hypotheses that attending school with advantaged classmates promotes learning in elementary school and high school graduation, delays sexual intercourse, lowers students' grades, and has no effect on high school seniors' chances of attending college. They say that having advantaged neighbors may encourage high school completion, increase teenagers' future earnings, and discourage teen pregnancy. Advantaged neighbors may lessen crime among affluent teenagers, but encourage it among poor teenagers, particularly if they are black.

One potentially important paper did find relatively large (if somewhat confusing) neighborhood effects. Corcoran and her colleagues (1987) find a large correlation between being raised in a neighborhood with a high proportion of welfare recipients and future poverty even after controlling for the families' own welfare use and other factors. But the impacts are not always consistent, and neighborhoods seem to have very different effects on welfare than on schooling or hours of work. An earlier paper by Linda Datcher (1982) used a similar methodology and also found some neighborhood effects.

Recently there has been a surge of literature seeking to measure neighborhood effects. Most of the papers find some such effects, but there is remarkably little consistency in them. J. Lawrence Aber et al. (1992) find them only for females; James Connell, Elizabeth Clifford, and Warren Crichlow (1992) only for males. Jeanne Brooks-Gunn et al. (1992) find them chiefly for high-income white girls; Connell and his colleagues see them mainly for low-income black males (though Brooks-Gunn et al. did not look at males). Aber and his colleagues find nothing for elementary school–aged children. Brooks-Gunn and her colleagues find effects for three-year-olds. Jonathon Crane (1991) found neighborhood effects on premarital fertility of black women. Lawrence Katz and Anne Case (1991) used tight definitions of neighborhoods and discovered peer effects on youth involvement in crime and drug use, and the probability that a young person will be out of school and out of work.

Far too small a fraction of the poor are found in very poor

neighborhoods to implicate concentration in the vast majority of cases of poverty, welfare use, and dependency. But for those areas where poverty is concentrated, there are certainly theoretical reasons to suspect adverse effects. Certainly it is plausible that neighborhood effects are important, and there is some evidence in support of the proposition. Current evidence is still too limited to draw firm conclusions. This area badly needs further research.

Intergenerational poverty and welfare use. The idea that poverty and welfare use are passed from one generation to the next because values of the parents are instilled in the child is a part of most cultural descriptions of poverty. But disadvantage can be linked across generations for reasons unrelated to values. Parents may not have the resources to provide a strong educational base for their children. Poor children may go to poor schools, may have less access to labor market contacts, and may suffer a variety of deprivations which put them at far greater risk of poverty without suffering from poor values. Parents pass much to their children genetically. Thus intergenerational correlation of poverty is a necessary but not sufficient condition for the cultural transmission of poverty.

We are again left with a limited literature that is subject to divergent interpretations. Lee Rainwater (1987) reports that 37.6 percent of poor children were later poor as adults. Of those who were not poor as children, 14.3 percent were poor as adults. He concludes that there is a solid association between poverty status as a child and poverty status as an adult, but notes that the majority of young adults who were poor had not been poor in childhood.

Various papers reach similar conclusions. But they often emphasize different points. That most poor persons did not themselves come from poor families is sometimes seen as disproving the intergenerational hypothesis, while the much higher probability of being poor among those who were poor as children is taken as confirmation.

Little work has been done to explore the links between welfare use across generations. Martha Hill and Michael Ponza (1986) show that 53 percent of black women who were raised in families with no welfare dependency (over the study period) avoided welfare themselves, while only 35 percent of those in families that received welfare avoided it in the future. Results for whites were equally large: 79 percent of white women with no welfare as a child had none during the study period when they were adults; 54 percent of women who grew up in homes with some welfare support got no welfare as adults. The study by Corcoran et al. (1987) found that children from families with heavy welfare use often fared much worse educationally or in the labor market.

But the empirical results often become unstable and peculiar when one tries to look further than the simple correlation between adult and child welfare receipt. For example, there were no consistent effects of the level of dependency on future welfare use among blacks in Hill and Ponza's results. Indeed, the data seem to show that black women raised in highly welfare dependent homes were less likely to be dependent on welfare than those raised in homes that received only a little welfare. Whites, by contrast, did seem to be affected in the predictable fashion by the level of past dependency. Corcoran and her colleagues also report confusing effects as level of dependency rises, and surprising interactions between a family's own welfare use and the overall level of welfare use in the neighborhood.

Sara McLanahan (1986) offers rather similar findings on the links between parental welfare receipt and the odds of becoming a female household head. Parental welfare receipt increases the chances of female headship, but the effect seems to get smaller as the level of parental welfare benefits rises (instead of the other way around). Results for familial welfare receipt on the employment of young men are also mixed, with Robert Lerman (1986) finding an effect and Hill and Ponza (1986) finding none.[5]

The really important question is not whether there are correlations in poverty or welfare across generations. It would be astounding to discover that there was complete economic mobility across generations. The issue, rather, is to what extent this correlation can be attributed to cultural and attitudinal factors as opposed to continuing disadvantage. On this matter the existing literature is quite limited. In one of the very few recent studies, Susan Chambre (1985) found no difference in attitudes about illegitimacy and pregnancy among first-generation welfare mothers, second-generation welfare users, and young mothers not on welfare.

The conclusion of Hill and Ponza and others seems to be that there is little evidence to support the cultural hypothesis for poverty and welfare use overall. The correlation across generations is actually smaller than many might have predicted, and the multivariate analyses often yield anomalous results with respect to the link between the amount of childhood dependency and the amount of adult dependency.

Our more cautious conclusion is that there is a modest connection across generations, but the causal links simply cannot be inferred from the available literature. Certainly we can reject the proposition that heavy dependency inevitably leads to dependency of the children because of the cultural links between parent and child. But just what, if any, cultural link can be found in the limited intergenerational correlation that has been reported cannot now be determined and may never be. This area deserves more careful research, especially in combination with work on concentration effects. But we will probably never be able to resolve whether the intergenerational effects are caused by the altered choices, confidence, or culture in poor and dependent homes.

Conclusions based on static results. On the basis of static information on work, welfare, and poverty problems alone, we may conclude that of the three models the choice framework seems most effective in explaining the results, but that there are enough anomalies in the data to warrant looking beyond the pure choice model. There is strong evidence that attitudes toward work and welfare have changed over time, though there is little evidence that the changes are related to a culture of poverty. And the fact that marital status plays an important predictive role is not easy to explain in the choice framework. Moreover, for those in severe poverty areas, concentration could be a significant influence. Still, the most direct tests of nonchoice models have to date been inconclusive.

Welfare Duration and Dynamics

The three explanations for dependence offer somewhat different predictions about welfare dynamics. The choice model suggests that earnings exits should be rare and that when they occur they ought to be closely linked to measures related to net earning capacity and incentives. The choice model is less clear about exits due to other reasons, but if welfare were quite dynamic, one would expect it to be because exits for reasons other than earnings were common. The choice model implicitly suggests that it would not become more difficult to leave welfare the longer one had been on the program.

The expectancy models suggest a more dynamic system. Some people ought to move off quickly. Others are likely to do so more slowly. And the longer one is on welfare, the harder it should be to get off, because confidence and self-esteem may decay with time in the system. Earnings exits would be more common if confidence and sense of control, rather than real options, were the main reason people stayed on welfare a long time. Noneconomic variables such as marital status are also expected to have some predictive power. This model could also be interpreted as predicting that returns to welfare will be common. People might try to make it on their own, but without some key social and economic supports, they will be easily knocked off their feet and then return to welfare.

The cultural models seem to suggest there ought to be two classes of people. Those who come onto welfare who were not raised in a "culture of poverty" ought to move off rather quickly, because their values are assumed to be inconsistent with long-term welfare use. Earnings exits ought to be common for these persons. For those who have been socialized in the ghetto or other areas of extreme deprivation, welfare would be expected to last a long time. Because choices are not the main reason people stay on welfare a long time, economic variables per se would not be so important except to the extent that they captured people's motivation and resolve. Let us look at the evidence.

Welfare duration. There is now a fair degree of consistency in findings about welfare durations. Studies such as O'Neill et al. (1984), Murray and Laren (1986), and Blank (1986) all come to surprisingly similar conclusions about welfare durations. These are all reviewed in detail in both Hoffman (1987) and Lerman (1986). Ellwood and Bane (see Chapter 2) present empirical findings consistent with this literature.

The median spell of welfare use is three years, yet the median total time on welfare is four years. The reason is that those who leave welfare often return. Thirty-five percent of those who leave welfare return for a second spell. Thus there are many people who escape welfare reasonably quickly, but half are on for over four years, and the high return rate suggests that staying off of welfare may not be easy. Almost one quarter of those who ever use AFDC end up collecting it in ten or more years, which is clear evidence that long-term welfare use affects a sizable minority (see Tables 2.1, 2.3).

Evidence from monthly data suggests even greater dynamics. The studies of Blank (1986), Gritz and McCurdy (1991), Harris (1992), Weeks (1991), and Pavetti (1993) all use monthly data and find shorter durations. All still find an important minority with very long stays. And they often find very high rates of recidivism. Pavetti, for example, finds that 70 percent who leave welfare for at least a month later return.

Generally the high degree of movement into and out of the welfare program seems somewhat inconsistent with a pure choice-based model. One would not expect frequent movements on and off of welfare in a world where basic opportunities and incentives were unchanged. Such movements suggest either misinformation, uncertainty, or a highly dynamic job market. If people find it hard to leave welfare permanently, however, then the lack of better choices may be the underlying problem that increased information reveals.

To distinguish among theories, we must also examine the reasons for the dynamics. If earnings and returning to welfare by those who have worked are quite common and only loosely linked to earning capacity, then the choice model looks less convincing. If the dynamics are created by variation in marriage or other factors, then we may look more favorably on the choice model.

Earnings exits from AFDC. Some earlier work suggested that earnings exits account for only a small portion of the exits from welfare. But, as noted in Chapter 2, more recent evidence suggests that earnings exits, at least short-term ones, are more common than previously reported. In the previous chapter, we concluded that perhaps as much as 40 percent of exits were for earnings. Blank (1986) reported 33 percent; Pavetti (1993), 45 percent; Gritz and McCurdy (1991), roughly half; Weeks (1991), 54 percent; and Harris (1992), nearly 70 percent. But it is important to note many of these earnings exits are short lived, sometimes lasting only a month or two. Pavetti reports that 65 percent of all who leave welfare for work return to welfare.

Conversely, a very large fraction of exits are not the result of earnings. By some classifications, the largest reason for leaving AFDC is marriage or reconciliation. And many people stay on AFDC until they lose eligibility for other reasons as well (see Table 2.8).

The factors that seem to influence which recipients earn their way off welfare can be predicted using an economic choice model. The factors that predict quick earnings exits are education, work experience, welfare payment level, and marital status. Age of the mother, number of children, and age of the youngest child have only a modest impact. Other than marital status, these are exactly the results one would expect based on the choice model. The economic variables are the most potent of all. Marital status has only a modest effect.

In sharp contrast, economic variables have very little power in predicting who leaves AFDC for other reasons, principally marriage. Education, work experience, and welfare payment levels have virtually no predictive power. The major predictors are marital status, age of youngest child, and number of children.

Taken at face value, these results suggest that earning capacity and incentives may have a fairly sizable effect on earnings exits, but that other factors influence marriage and the other routes out of AFDC. Education influences welfare duration by improving the odds that someone will earn her way off of welfare. Marital status influences durations through a modest impact on the odds that someone will leave with high earnings and a large impact on other exits.

These results give mixed support to choice and expectancy models. That traditional economic variables predict durations and earnings exits reasonably well supports the choice theory. To explain the significance of education and previous work experience using expectancy or cultural models, one has to argue that these are capturing the effects of confidence, ambition, and traditional values. Those with confidence or mainstream values worked harder in school and in the labor market. But if education and work experience are correlated with confidence and positive values, it is hard to see why these have little measured effect on nonearnings exits such as marriage.

But the relatively high level of earnings exits and the frequency of returns to welfare strongly suggest that something else is going on. Women are going to work in spite of the poor work incentives, but they are apparently unable to sustain that work. This seems quite inconsistent with the choice theory. This behavior only seems consistent with poor information and great uncertainty in people's lives. No static choice model can explain such a high level of dynamics in work.

Still, that earnings exits are so hard to sustain is probably support for the choice story. Apparently women go to work, hoping to be able to get off welfare, only to come face to face with the realities of their opportunities and choices. Thus one might explain this result as being supportive of the underlying pressures and incentives found in the choice framework, coupled with the uncertainty and complexity emphasized by expectancy theories. Choice or expectancy models alone seem unable to explain the data. If both models are at work, then the inability of women to sustain work has worrisome implications. Expectancy models suggest that after a series of failures to leave welfare, women become discouraged and stop trying.

This relatively high level of dynamics seems most inconsistent with cultural theories. The relatively high rate of going to work seems prima facie evidence of a desire to work, especially in the face of weak work incentives. Still, the level of dynamics can be overstated. A sizable fraction never appear to go to work. An important part of the caseload stays on welfare continuously for many years.

Evidence on heterogeneity versus state dependence in welfare use. One area where the models provide clearly different predictions is in the effects of duration of dependence on welfare exits. Choice models suggest that it ought to be just about as hard for people to leave welfare in their first year as in their tenth. The other models suggest that either confidence or values are likely to decay with time on welfare and that people will become trapped. One can, in principle, test the proposition that it becomes increasingly difficult to leave welfare using methodological techniques now being applied to longitudinal data by economists and others seeking to separate "heterogeneity" and "state dependence."

Although the methodologies are often complex, the basic idea behind such methods is relatively easy to understand. If welfare traps people, then the odds of leaving welfare ought to decline with time on the program. Thus a natural test is to see whether the exit rate from welfare decreases as time on the program increases.

Appearances can be deceiving, however. If one looks at a heterogeneous group of people who differ in their chances of escape, one would expect the *group's* odds of leaving welfare to diminish as time on welfare rose, even if the odds stayed constant for each individual. In the early years, the group on welfare will include both people who are likely to move off quickly and people who are slow to get off. So the average exit rate for the group will be high. In later years only the slow-to-leave people will be left on welfare, so the average rate of escape for the *remaining* group will be low even if no individual has changed. The make-up of the group has changed, creating the illusion that exit rates are falling.

Still, an obvious place to start is to find out whether exit rates decline as time on welfare increases. If they do, then the far more complex determination of whether the declines reflect heterogeneity or state dependence begins. If they do not decline, one must be skeptical that severe "welfare dependence" is present, because heterogeneity alone should cause exit rates to decline.

Exit rates for welfare recipients as a whole do decline as time on welfare increases (see Table 2.1 for our estimates of the rates). Rebecca Blank (1986), who used a different data set from the one that generated the exit rates reported in Chapter 2, also concluded that there was little evidence of state dependence in welfare. Yet another study, using a different methodology and looking at the evidence from the Seattle and Denver income maintenance experiments, concluded, "the evidence pointing towards a welfare trap is at best weak" (Plant 1984, p. 682).

An alternative method of testing for such dependence is to look and see if attitudes and sense of control seem to decline with time on welfare. Hill et al. (1985) found little support for such a hypothesis in data from the Panel Study of Income Dynamics. Goodwin (1983), however, suggests that there may be some effect. In general, there is surprisingly little statistical evidence so far to support the notion of a welfare trap.

If this evidence is to be believed, it provides one of the strongest sources of evidence that welfare does not rob people of confidence and self-esteem. Yet the evidence needs to be considered in the light of previous findings. Earnings exits ought to be the route out of welfare that falls off rapidly. Because earnings exits are such a small proportion of the total, rather sizable changes in earnings patterns might be lost if other exit rates are stable.

Conclusions based on dynamic results. The results here, as in the static case, are open to many interpretations. Certainly the high degree of dynamics, including frequent exits and returns to welfare, argues against static models such as the choice model. And the consistency of marital status as one of the most powerful predictors of duration seems to point toward models emphasizing confidence or culture. Nor do the reasonably high level of earnings exits point toward a choice model.

Yet consistent with the choice models, the factors that explain exits in general and work exits in particular are closely related to economic opportunity and choices. Persons whom one would expect to do better in the labor market leave more often. And the high rate of recidivism might best be seen as evidence that choices are poor.

Perhaps most surprising of all, there is little evidence to date from either statistical or attitudinal work that people really become trapped on welfare in the sense that it becomes harder and harder to escape as duration on the program increases. Finding that some people spend ten or even twenty years on welfare seems to prove that people become trapped. They remain on welfare a long, long time. Yet they may be stuck there as much because they lack alternatives as because they have become passive or unmotivated. The most appropriate conclusion is that a joint choice/expectancy model, in which recipients face great uncertainty and complexity in their lives along with a very weak set of choices, is the only one consistent with the data.

Policy Initiatives in Work and Welfare

One of the places where the models diverge the most is in policy focus. Choice models emphasize program incentives and training options designed to make work more financially attractive. Expectancy models suggest that we ought to understand the human side of welfare and find ways to increase the confidence and perceived control of those on welfare. Cultural models are often used to suggest that we ought to impose rules and restrictions on those in welfare. Let us briefly review the evidence.

The impact of program incentives. A very large body of research has explored the way in which program incentives influence work behavior. These have consistently and uniformly shown that social welfare programs do influence work hours in a way consistent with the choice perspective of economic theory. Robert Moffitt's (1992) summary of the literature suggests that those then on AFDC would have increased their hours of work from an average of nine hours per week to perhaps fourteen hours if the program were abolished, which implies that the program reduced work by 30 percent. Still, according to this estimate, even in the absence of the program, work hours would still be very low and families quite poor. Results of the negative income tax experiments summarized by Gary Burtless (1987) show that a 10 percent increase in income leads to a 2 percent reduction in work by single parents. Unfortunately there are no findings available to examine the impact of program characteristics on dependency and work behavior over many years.

Work incentives in the form of marginal tax rates or benefit reduction rates seem to have very little impact. Those who predicted massive changes in work when the Reagan administration and Congress eliminated "30 and 1/3" from AFDC (so that welfare recipients now lose $1 in benefits for each dollar earned) were surprised to find very modest impacts. Thus it appears to some observers that single parents do not respond to economic incentives.

This finding can be taken as a repudiation of the economic choice paradigm. But the choice models can explain the small impact of varying benefit reduction rates. Changing the rates has two offsetting effects. On the one hand, the reward for working is higher, leading people to want to work more. On the other hand, those who are already working get to keep more money (making them better off at the same level of work effort), which makes them want to work less. The empirical results consistently show that these "substitution" and "income" effects are almost exactly equal in magnitude, so that the overall response is small. Moreover, Frank Levy (1979), Robert Moffitt (1985), Charles Murray (1984), and others have all pointed out that reducing the benefit reduction rate will make more people eligible for welfare and the work effort of these newly eligible persons will be unambiguously reduced.

Single parents do respond in predictable ways to changing incentives. But the empirical work reviewed suggests that the impacts are modest. Moffitt (1992, p. 13) is even more emphatic: "employment rates and hours of work of female heads have been extraordinarily stable . . . despite major changes in benefit levels, benefit reduction rates, benefit-earnings rations, and unemployment rates. . . . This extreme inelasticity does not augur well for the prospect of increasing work by any change in benefits or benefit-reduction rates."

This is not a repudiation of choice-based models. Even relatively large changes in benefit formulas may do little to alter the basic choices people face. We have noted that wives rarely pick the full-year full-time work option even though the economic disincentives to doing so are far smaller for them than for those eligible for welfare. "Reasonable" people often choose to stay home with their families even absent adverse incentives. But the results clearly suggest that modest changes in benefit policy (either liberalizing or tightening) in the range countenanced in relevant political debate are unlikely to have major impacts on work and dependency. Other policy directions may be more fruitful.

The administrative and human side of welfare. The expectancy models suggest that the administrative and human side of welfare may have far more to do with people's success than with program incentives. Bane and Michael Dowling (1985) argue that administrative practices have far more effect on caseload levels than incentives do, though the evidence seems fragmentary. In part, they claim, administrators and recipients may see welfare as a program for those who don't work, thus reinforcing welfare dependency. Michael Sosin (1986) summarizes a large literature that explores the links between administrative practices, caseloads, and the treatment of recipients.

Closely related is the literature on the human side of welfare. Welfare receipt involves far more than a grant and a benefit reduction rate. There is a large case study literature that reveals that welfare clients are often humiliated and belittled (Piven and Cloward 1971; Handler 1972; Stack 1974; Goodban 1985). There have been dramatic changes in the way in which welfare is administered, moving from a caseworker approach in the 1960s to a more bureaucratic approach today (see Chapter 1). But under both systems the clients often report feeling abused, isolated, and helpless.

Rules and regulations are so complex that administrators often report that welfare recipients do not understand what their options and rights are. The marginal incentives are even more confusing, particularly with differing rules across many different programs. The experience of welfare may be far more one of dealing with stigmatization, bureaucratic rules, and conflicting signals than one of income guarantees and marginal tax rates.

Thus there is considerable case study and anecdotal evidence that the administrative and human side of the welfare system has a great deal to do with recipients' behavior. Yet this is not necessarily evidence that expectancy theories of dependency are valid. Expectancy theories do not only imply that welfare imposes adverse rules, bureaucracy, and stigmatization. They also suggest that as a result, people are less able to become independent and that they lose confidence and become "helpless." Evidence that welfare is a very unpleasant, "dehumanizing" experience is not proof that the treatment creates dependency. Indeed a reasonable hypothesis might be that bad treatment at the hands of the welfare system increases the incentive to achieve independence.

There are some authors who argue that by comparing practices across offices or by exploring the actual situation of clients one can infer that system characteristics play an important role in creating or discouraging dependency. Mead (1986) claims that the attitudes and expectations of administrators have a great effect on recipients' work effort, but his evidence is not particularly strong. Frances Fox Piven and Richard Cloward (1971) claim the welfare system is specifically designed to create a more docile lower class, which thus loses its ability to make demands on the system. But here, too, hard evidence is difficult to come by. This area merits further research. For now there is no clear evidence that making the system more humane or intelligible will greatly diminish dependency, desirable as such changes might be for other reasons.

The role of supports such as day care, medical protection, and child support. The different models of dependency predict different levels of importance for benefits such as day care, medical services, or child support. In the cultural framework, they are relatively unimportant. People who want to work find a way to do so. In the choice framework, having to pay for day care and medical protection adds to the costs of working and reduces the attractiveness of work over welfare. In the expectancy model, fears about day care and medical costs may be so serious that the availability or lack of such supports may have a far greater impact than their pure financial value.

The treatment of day care in the literature is generally quite weak. We do not know much about how day-care needs affect use of work and welfare. Formal day care remains uncommon. As of 1985, only 28 percent of single mothers with young children used an organized day-care facility, though the share is growing. Relatives, most often grandmothers, provided care for 42 percent of these cases (U.S. Census 1987, table 1, p. 13). Relatives are often unavailable, however. The evidence suggests that the majority of working-age grandmothers are themselves in the labor force. Other forms of care cost more, often a considerable sum. Denise Polit and Joseph O'Hara (1989) review the evidence on the importance of child care for welfare recipients seeking to enter employment. They conclude that existing evidence, though limited, does support the argument that child-care services promote self-sufficiency. This finding is consistent with both the choice and the expectancy theories. This area urgently needs more comprehensive work.

Only a few studies have examined the role that lack of medical coverage plays in dependency. Using a sample covering four states, Blank (1989) found little evidence that the state level of Medicaid benefits had any significant influence on participation, but Moffitt and Barbara Wolfe (1989) found strong evidence that lack of private insurance increased AFDC participation. They predict that the AFDC caseload would drop 16 percent if all working female heads had insurance coverage equivalent to Medicaid. Anne Winkler (1991) reports disincentive effects of state Medicaid benefits on female-head labor supply. Ellwood and Kathleen Adams (1990) find that people with high expected medical costs are less likely to leave welfare. They conclude that the loss of Medicaid associated with leaving welfare probably does have an important deterrent effect on welfare exits, as choice theory predicts.

Child support is a different kind of supplementary benefit. Choice models suggest that it ought to have the same effect on work as any other nonwork source of income, such as welfare. It does have the major advantage that it comes without a benefit reduction rate— child support benefits are not taken away as earnings increase, the way welfare is. But the expectancy model and some cultural models imply that child support may be seen as something very different from welfare. Because it comes without the need of going through the welfare system and because it has no stigma associated to it, child support could in principle be empowering in a way that welfare never could. Current evidence, however, suggests that dealing with the child-support system may be just as frustrating, isolating, and discouraging as working with the welfare system. Indeed the two systems are often partially integrated.

In a review paper, Lerman (1987) indicates that we know relatively little about the way in which various child-support options are likely to influence welfare use. The evidence to date does not seem to support a view that child support is different from other outside sources of income. By itself, child support seems unlikely to move many women off of welfare, because payments rarely exceed welfare benefit levels. What is unknown, though, is whether a more stable and reliable source of outside income could serve as a base that welfare mothers could supplement with their own earnings to achieve greater self-support. This is an area of intense interest, debate, and experimentation among states.

One program not already discussed is New York State's Child Assistance Program (CAP). It offered a much more generous support system to women who had child-support awards in place and who were working. The result was that work did increase significantly and child-support awards shot up. Yet the impact varied by county. In sites where the CAP office was separated from the welfare office, participants did much better than at locations where the CAP program was run out of the welfare office. Under the choice model this result is anomalous, because the incentives were the same. But administrators and recipients reported that when CAP was separated from the welfare office, recipients perceived it as an alternative—a way off of welfare—and thus were much more motivated to use it. Moreover, program administrators strongly emphasized the need to provide a variety of support services for CAP recipients to succeed (Hamilton et al. 1992).

In the CAP program the incentives did seem to work, but only when they were accompanied by a change in the nature of the program and by other supports. This one success may have been sustained by a combination of better choices and measures to change the nature of support. And even here, the vast majority of people eligible for CAP did not choose it.

Voluntary employment and training programs. Choice models suggest that training is critical to enhance people's options in the labor market. Expectancy models also suggest that in building self-confidence, realistic expectations are quite important. Employment and training programs have tried both to build skills and to increase confidence through a variety of methods.

Program initiatives in this area include classroom training in both basic and job-related skills, job clubs to provide mutual support to those seeking employment, work experience programs, and on-the-job training. Supported Work initiatives have attempted to ease the transition to private sector employment (Grossman, Maynard, and Roberts 1985).

These programs have had some success, and often have their greatest impact on the hardest to employ. Yet all of these programs have had only a modest impact in reducing dependency. The work-welfare demonstrations, which mostly involved job clubs and work experience programs, rarely increased average earnings by more than $600 per year. Welfare savings were much smaller. Even Supported Work—which showed larger gains and was very expensive—reduced the fraction of people receiving welfare two years after the program from 85 percent to only about 70 percent.

Mandatory work initiatives. Conservative proponents of cultural theories often suggest mandatory work programs to overcome what they see as a subculture of dependency that rejects the mainstream work ethic. In recent years there have been a number of programs that required participation in some form from at least a subset of recipients. The Manpower Demonstration Research Corporation (MDRC) evaluated a limited mandatory work program for recipients in San Diego and found that those who worked generally found work requirements fair and reasonable (Gueron 1986; Friedlander and Gueron 1990). In the words of one researcher quoted in the report, "We did not invent the work ethic, we found it."

Others, such as Mickey Kaus (1986) and Mead (1986), point to low levels of actual participation in such mandatory work programs, asserting that people who want to escape participation can do so. If only those who want to work are found in mandatory jobs, then it is not surprising that they are satisfied with them. Kaus claims that work-welfare programs have been a failure at compelling work and that "only work works" in undoing the mother-child subculture of poverty.

There seems to be no evidence with which to judge Kaus's assertion. Critics are correct in asserting that "hard workfare," in which every recipient works for her welfare check, has not been tried in the major federal programs, though some state general assistance programs come close. But no evidence exists that "hard workfare" affects attitudes or motivation.

There is, however, some evidence that programs that seek to move welfare recipients into work quickly can be more successful. The most successful site in the California GAIN program strongly emphasized that people work as soon as possible. This county had the highest impacts observed in any MDRC work-welfare demonstration. That the program emphasized the critical need to move people into work quickly indicates that something more than choice issues is involved. More traditional education investments were more strongly emphasized in other programs, but these were less successful (Riccio and Friedlander 1992).

Similarly Toby Herr, Robert Halpern, and Aimee Conrad (1991) also emphasize that a "work first, educate later" approach seems to work better with long-term recipients. They argue that recipients only determine that education is important after being out in the job market and discovering that what they aspire to requires more education.

These last bits of evidence are intriguing. Although there is still too little data to reach firm conclusions, it points again to a situation in which both motivation and information are very important. Educational programs will do little good for people unmotivated to learn. Some recipients apparently need to be "pushed" to go to work—carrots alone are not enough.

Recent evidence from the LEAP program in Ohio is also revealing. Teenage AFDC recipients were given a large bonus to stay in school and suffered a large benefit cut if they failed to do so. The initial results were dramatic. This appears to provide powerful evidence for an incentive-based (choice) strategy. Yet researchers claimed that the existence of a counseling and support program was a necessary ingredient for the success of the program (Bloom et al. 1993).

Conclusions based on policy experiences. Until recently, policy experiments seemed to leave us in a frustrating position. On the one hand, the interventions made a positive difference. On the other hand, results were often frustratingly modest. One frustrating feature is that none of the obvious policy levers linked to the welfare system that had been investigated seemed likely to have more than a modest effect on long-term welfare use. The fact that none had shown a large effect cannot be used to accept or reject any of the models. All the models suggest that modest changes in policy are likely to have moderate effects on behavior, especially in the short run.

Yet more recent results offer a glimmer of hope. Mixed models— those that combine incentives and social support and even pressure to go to work or school immediately—appear to be working somewhat better. It is difficult to draw firm conclusions here, but the choice model alone cannot explain the patterns we observe. Confidence, expectations, and motivation all appear to play some role. Especially for programs targeted at long-term recipients, program administrators often report that social and other supports are every bit as important as the incentives people face.

What remains very clear, however, is that most existing work programs have not shown a profound impact, whether they are designed to be punitive or supportive. Claims that the work ethic has been lost and that enforced work will put it back have not been demonstrated. Neither does evidence support the assertion that work rules are unnecessary as long as jobs are available.

Evidence on the Factors Influencing Family Structure

The three models offer rather different predictions about family structure: the choice model suggests that economic variables such as welfare benefits and the earnings of men and women are likely to play a key role. Expectancy and informational models suggest that at least some family decisions, especially those of never-married mothers, may be influenced by a sense of isolation and lack of control in other aspects of life. And cultural theories tend to point to a change in attitudes, arising most prominently in areas of concentrated poverty.

One of the more intriguing aspects of the current debate is that liberals often claim that labor market choices available to men in particular have played an important role in shaping family behavior, but they reject the view that welfare could have played much of a role. Conservatives adopt an opposite view. In principle, the choice model suggests that both the labor market and welfare could have played a role, and that if one economic factor is important, another is likely to be as well.

The research in this area is less complete and less convincing than in the areas already discussed. Because the research is often focused on one or another factor, it is reviewed here by examining the findings on the several influences that have gotten the most attention.

The impact of welfare benefits. In popular debate, welfare is often treated as the primary culprit responsible for the recent sharp increases in the proportion of children living in poor single-parent families. There is a fairly sizable body of research in this area, but the decisions involved are so complex that methodological compromises are made in every study and the results seem to vary depending on the empirical methods used. Thus those with strongly held views can generally find results to support their position and find some legitimate basis for criticizing studies that do not support their position (Garfinkel and McLanahan 1986; Wilson and Neckerman 1986).

The only true experimental evidence comes from the Negative Income Tax (NIT) experiments. Lyle Groeneveld, Michael Hannan, and Nancy Tuma (1983) report negative effects on the marital stability of those who were in the experimental groups relative to the controls. These results have been sharply criticized in a careful reanalysis of the same data by Glen Cain (1987), who argues the earlier results were misleading, unstable, and inconclusive. In any case the results are of questionable value in understanding the impact of the current system, because the experimentals received new benefits and the controls were in the present system. Moreover, the experimental and short-term nature of the NIT makes results suspect. Still, this is one piece of evidence that economic choices can affect family structure decisions.

Other work has used various modeling techniques to exploit non-experimental data. Generally the variation in welfare benefits across states is used as a kind of natural experiment for testing the impact of welfare benefits. Two basic approaches have been taken. Some authors (Danziger et al. [1982] provide the best-known example) have tried to create a structural choice model of marital choices. Others, such as Ellwood and Bane (1985), use reduced form estimates. Both approaches in the literature have, at least until recently, shown weak effects for welfare, or the results have been so sensitive to empirical assumptions that they were not very credible.

Yet there are clear hints that economic factors have some impact.

For example, both Danziger et al. (1982) and Ellwood and Bane (1985) report that welfare has some effect on behavior. The latter work suggests that welfare's impact inversely is proportional to the significance of the event. There is little observed impact of welfare on births out of wedlock. There is a larger impact on the decision of women to divorce. Impacts are particularly sizable on the decision of a woman who is already a single parent to live in her parent(s)' home. Still, considering the amount of press potential welfare effects receive, it is remarkable that so few studies have found large effects.

It is important to remember that most of the earlier work, including the studies just cited, is based on data from 1975 and earlier. More recent research, notably that of Laurie Bassi (1987), has sometimes found a larger effect. One crucial fact, nevertheless, must be explained by anyone attempting to use changed welfare benefits as a primary explanation for changes in family structure: the temporal patterns of welfare benefit changes do not correspond well to the temporal pattern of family structure changes.

According to the House Committee on Ways and Means, between 1960 and 1972 welfare benefits were raised dramatically. The combined weighted state average AFDC plus food stamp benefits for a family of four measured in 1986 dollars rose from $7,066 in 1960 to $9,359 in 1972. And these figures understate the true change, because Medicaid benefits were added and eligibility rules were liberalized. But since 1972, benefits have fallen sharply. In 1986 they averaged $7,519—a fall of over 20 percent since their peak in 1972, and a real increase of only 6 percent since 1960. The situation was better than it had been in 1960, because all recipients got Medicaid and some had some housing and other forms of assistance. But there is no doubt that the disposable income available to welfare mothers fell considerably between 1972 and 1986 (U.S. House, Ways and Means 1987, p. 662).[6]

As a result of these cutbacks, even though the number of children in female-headed families grew by three million between 1972 and 1984,[7] and even though the economy was much worse (unemployment higher and real wages lower) in 1984, the number of children on AFDC actually fell by over half a million (U.S. House, Ways and Means 1987, pp. 429–430).

The problem with using welfare in a choice model is that it cannot explain all the growth in single-parent families since 1972. It is difficult to make the case that women were increasingly choosing welfare over marriage during a period when benefits were falling and the number of children on welfare was falling, rather than rising, as the choice model would predict. Thus while there is some evidence that welfare influences family choices modestly, the evidence to date does not strongly support the choice-based models.

The impact of men's and women's earnings. Both the sociological theories championed by Talcott Parsons (Parsons and Bales, 1955) and the economic theories of Gary Becker (1973, 1981) suggest that marriage may be a more likely choice when there is greater division and specialization of labor. One interpretation of choice models, therefore, is that the pattern of forming and maintaining intact families with "traditional" roles will be strengthened by increases in men's earning capacity and weakened by increases in women's earning capacity.

In expectancy models, an increase in earnings by men generally appears to promote intact families, but the impact of increased earnings by women is unclear. The higher earnings of men would seem to increase the confidence and control of the husband and thus strengthen the family. Increased earnings by women would also seem to increase a woman's confidence and control. Because lack of confidence and control is often seen as an important influence on illegitimacy, one might expect out-of-wedlock births to fall with increased women's earnings. But they might also create more tension, and could offer women a chance for control that would allow them to escape an unhappy marriage.

In cultural models, work is often treated as universally good, because it helps to reinforce the work ethic. But some conservatives worry that the absence of a parent at home may hurt the children.

This question is another on which the literature is rather thin. There have been a variety of studies that have looked at the relation between male joblessness and marriage and divorce. The most prominent recent work has been done by William Julius Wilson and his colleagues. Wilson and Katherine Neckerman (1986) note that the ratio of employed black men to all young black women has declined significantly in the past few decades. The decline closely parallels similar declines in the marriage rates of blacks generally. It offers one of the few explanations that is consistent with the time-series evidence. Mark Testa (1990), however, found that male job-lessness cannot fully explain the decline of black marriage rates, and Richard Mare and Christopher Winship (1991) estimate that changes in employment can explain only about 20 percent of the decline in the marriage rates of young black men since 1960.

Ellwood and Jonathon Crane (1990) conclude that economic models have not been very successful in explaining the changes in black or white families. Ellwood and David Rodda (1991), using a hazard model methodology to examine trends in male employment and marriage rates during the last two decades, find that changes in employment patterns are relatively modest compared with the dra-matic declines in marriage, especially among black men. Thus, al-though they find strong evidence that work and earnings influence the marriage patterns of young men, they conclude that changes in employment can explain only a small fraction of the decline in marriage for both black and white men.

There is some evidence that unemployment influences divorce and marital instability. For example, Heather Ross and Isabel Sawhill (1975) find that divorce is more common in homes in which the husband has been unemployed. And Saul Hoffman and Greg Duncan (1986) find that marriage prospects have some influence on remarriage, though the effects are small, especially for blacks. This literature thus hints that male earning patterns may play a modest role overall and could play a large role for certain subgroups.

The literature regarding women's employment is similar, point-ing toward some effects, but without definitive results. Several stud-ies, notably that of Sam Preston and Alan Richards (1975), have suggested that where opportunities for women are greater, marriage rates are lower. And as families adjust to the new roles of men and women, work may introduce a new source of stress in families. Several studies suggest that husbands sometimes have lower self-esteem in households in which the wife works (e.g., Kessler and McRae [1982]). Catherine Ross, John Mirowsky, and John Huber (1983) report that stress seems to be mostly confined to couples in which the woman is working for financial reasons and the couples believe it would be better if the woman stayed home. Ross and Sawhill (1975) report that the odds of divorce rise as the earnings of the wife rise relative to the husband. Ross and Sawhill and others have also shown an association between employment opportunities and nonmarital childbearing.

Overall, one can conclude only that the existing literature indicates that earnings of men and women have some impact on family structure events. But the literature is neither detailed enough nor reliable enough to allow many conclusions about the logic of different models based on this information, because all models suggest some link between men's and women's earnings and family decisions.

Changing attitudes and values. Cultural and expectancy models both suggest that people's attitudes and perceptions ought to play a major role in family structure decisions. Choice models often treat such preferences as given. There is significant evidence that attitudes have changed over time, though whether these are the cause or effect of changed behavior remains controversial.

Sexual mores, for example, have clearly changed. Irwin Garfinkel and Sara McLanahan (1986, p. 82) summarize some of the evidence: "Two surveys carried out by the National Opinion Research Center . . . indicate that the proportion of adults who believed in total sexual abstinence before marriage dropped from 80 percent in 1963 to only 30 percent in 1975. The shift in attitudes was even greater among college students. The proportion of students who believed in total sexual abstinence for unmarried women dropped from 55 percent in 1967 to about 11 percent in the early 1970s."

There were sharp increases in reported premarital sexual activity. Almost half (48 percent) of first-time brides in the period 1960–1964 claimed that they did not have intercourse before marriage. Only about one quarter (28 percent) of new brides ten years later made the same claim. By the eighties the figure appeared to be below 20 percent (U.S. Census 1985c, table 99, p. 64). No figures are available on male virginity.

There are persistent claims in the press that attitudes toward giving birth to a child out of wedlock have softened over time.

According to one survey in 1974, only 31 percent of women agreed with the statement, "There is no reason why single women shouldn't have children and raise them if they want to." By 1985, 49 percent agreed. Other surveys show less favorable reactions (Zelnick, Kanter, and Ford 1981). Some evidence exists that attitudes toward single parenthood are more positive in ghetto areas. And Americans definitely do not see an imposed marriage as the solution for a single woman who is about to have a baby. In 1985 only about 20 percent of Americans agreed that "a couple having a child out of wedlock should marry for the sake of the child even though they don't want to" (Roper Organization, n.d.).

Attitudes about divorce have also changed. Andrew Cherlin notes that surveys showed that in 1968, 60 percent of adults thought divorce should be made "more difficult to obtain." In 1978, even after divorce laws had been liberalized considerably, only 42 percent thought divorce should be tougher (Cherlin 1981, p. 48). Divorce is seen as a legitimate option by the large majority of Americans as of 1985. In one 1985 survey, roughly 60 percent of adults say they favor divorce if "a marriage isn't working out." Another 20 percent or so say it depends (Roper Organization, n.d.).

It is very clear that attitudes have changed. Some changes might be explained as a response to altered choices. But it seems very difficult to explain most in a choice framework. Yet these changes need not be the result of lack of confidence or ghetto culture. Indeed the fact that college students show the greatest changes in sexual mores suggests that these alterations in attitude have been brought on by forces far removed from personal failure or ghetto culture.

Evidence on teenage pregnancy. Teenage pregnancy is justifiably a source of particular concern. To the casual observer, the teenage years seem to be a time when confidence and culture (in the form of peer pressure) play a strong role and rational thought is often absent. The evidence on teenage pregnancy seems to support this interpretation.

The most comprehensive report to date has come from the National Academy of Sciences (Hayes 1987). The report suggests a pattern of behavior in which low self-perception, poor achievement, peer influence, and parental attitudes work together to influence sexual behavior. It concludes that adolescents' "attitudes about sexual behavior, contraception, abortion, marriage, and single parenthood" are very important factors, though it finds that the origins of such attitudes are extremely complex. Moreover, it notes: "Several studies of social and psychological factors associated with adolescents' sexual behavior conclude that self-perception (not self-esteem)—that is, what and who one is, can be, and wants to be—is at the heart of teenagers' sexual decision making" (Hayes 1987, p. 120).

The report strongly emphasizes many factors that the expectancy and cultural models predict will be important. It notes a lack of knowledge and thought regarding contraceptive use. And it points to a very strong link between sexual behavior and both achievements and expected future achievements. A number of other studies suggest a strong association between low intellectual ability, low academic achievement, a lack of educational goals, and early sexual experience among both blacks and whites (Hayes 1987, p. 100).

The existing evidence shows quite clearly that a narrow choice model cannot be used to understand teenagers' behavior with respect to sexuality and fertility. Broader models seem essential here, including ones where behavior is related to a sense of future choices, to self-perception, and to peer and family attitudes.

Conclusions on family structure. There is evidence that factors such as welfare or male and female wages and unemployment have some influence on family structure. And in a few cases, such as the work of Wilson, there are indications that the influence may be strong. Generally, though, economic and choice models have done a modest job at best of explaining the changes in family structure. Indeed, the previous sections showed that while economic variables are very effective at predicting who will leave welfare with high earnings, they are far less effective in predicting exits for other reasons. Yet the evidence is not particularly strong that any model can really explain marriage and fertility patterns. Attitudes and self-perceptions are obviously important, but it is not clear that either expectancy or cultural models can be used to understand family structure changes. With research indicating that the typical child born in

America today will spend some time in a single-parent home, it is hard to believe that confidence or ghetto culture models capture the primary forces.

Generally the family structure results prove more than anything a need for more research. It appears that no simple model will take us very far here. Behavior seems influenced by choices and individual attitudes and perceptions. Thus the call ought to be for research that employs more sophisticated models incorporating several disciplines.

Conclusions from the Research

The evidence has led us to the rather inevitable conclusion: no single model works best for all circumstances. Still, we can do more than simply report that this is a complicated problem.

Static and Dynamic Welfare Use

Earlier versions of this review noted how well the choice model seemed to explain the data. But more recent information indicates more limitations of the choice-based model alone. There is no reading of the evidence that sustains a conclusion that choices, incentives, and opportunity are unimportant. The choice model suggested that mixing work and welfare should be uncommon, that it ought to be difficult for people to earn their way off of welfare, and that variables linked to earning potential should be the most prominent in explaining earnings exits when they did occur. Mixing work and welfare (legally) has indeed been rare. A majority of exits are probably not related to work. And when earnings exits do occur, they have been closely linked to characteristics that influenced the earning capacity of the person.

Looking at the options available to many single mothers, it is not surprising to find that long-term welfare use affects an important minority of those who ever use welfare. Most single mothers face a difficult choice: work all the time or be on welfare. Moreover, even if people choose to work full-time, they often will be only slightly better off than if they stayed on welfare. Many women therefore use welfare.

There are important patterns in the data that a choice model alone cannot explain, however. Earnings exits were higher than would be predicted. Perhaps more important, there are more short-term exits and returns than one would expect in a pure choice model. The high level of dynamics and recidivism suggests much more complexity, misinformation, and uncertainty than is usually assumed in static choice models. Nor do choice models explain the relative significance of marital status—especially being never-married—on welfare dynamics. And the recent surge in caseloads apparently cannot be readily explained by economic changes.

The evidence directly related to the expectancy models was decidedly mixed. There is little direct evidence that attitudes or expectations are playing a major role. Although there is considerable affirmation that welfare can intimidate, isolate, and stigmatize, existing statistical evidence so far does not point strongly toward a welfare trap. Still, research using nonchoice models was far more limited and far more difficult to interpret. It seems ludicrous to argue that motivation and self-worth are not linked closely to behavior, especially behavior on welfare. There seems no question that welfare can leave women feeling powerless and passive. And there is a growing literature showing that in some circumstances, when poor persons are given more control over their housing or some other feature in their life, they respond by taking on new responsibilities and gaining new confidence to move into other areas.

The cultural models performed least well. The fact that less than 10 percent of welfare recipients live in ghettos suggests that the bulk of the welfare problem cannot be attributed to problems in the streets. There is some evidence that poverty in ghettos, though small in proportion to the whole, is different in important ways. Whether the problem is that choices are much worse there because quality education and well-paying jobs are not found in ghettos or whether the problem is more the result of isolation and distorted values, however, is not truly known. And if isolation has distorted attitudes and expectations, we don't truly know what forces shaped those attitudes. Outside of ghetto communities, though, the evidence linking dependence primarily to confidence or culture is weak.

We need more research that uses the expectancy and cultural models, but in ways other than trying to measure attitudes and expectations. Expectancy models suggest that factors such as medical coverage, day care, and even the attitudes of workers may be critical in helping people escape welfare. Cultural models point to the critical role of concentrated poverty and isolation in creating long-term disadvantage. These issues can and should be researched. And one ought to be able to extend choice-based models at least to allow for some endogeneity of tastes and preferences. Ultimately fuller models of behavior are necessary to understand dependency. At present, it should be clear that a large part of the evidence on long-term welfare use can be understood without resorting to models emphasizing lack of confidence or adverse values.

Policy Interventions

Here too the emerging evidence has forced some reexamination. One of the most discouraging findings of this research is that neither long-term welfare use nor family structure changes seem to have been much influenced by moderate changes in policy. And all of the models pointed to the modest impacts of any policy. The estimated behavioral responses for welfare use under a choice model were small enough to suggest that even large changes in benefit levels and tax rates would create only limited changes in behavior. Employment and training programs have modest effects. Programs designed to provide peer support help somewhat. Programs with aggressive rules about participation make some difference. But as long as the programs look roughly as they do now, there seems little evidence that welfare rolls would be sharply reduced or increased if either the pragmatic liberal or the conservative agenda were adopted.

In part the policy dilemma is a function of the complexity of behavior as consequential as childbearing, welfare use, work, marriage, and fertility. These behaviors involve such strong feelings that they cannot be easily influenced by the kind of limited policy changes the body politic is prone to adopt.

Nevertheless, the review offers clear evidence that policy changes can make some difference and that the different paradigms for behavior offer clear ideas for testing potential policies. Increasingly, the literature suggests that a mixture of improved and altered incentives with a variety of support services may be the most effective intervention strategy. Just as neither the choice nor expectancy model alone can explain all of welfare dynamics, neither incentives nor supportive services seem to work effectively in isolation.

The second generation of welfare reforms is now under way. The most successful ones appear to stress moving quickly to work or education, rewarding desirable behavior, and often sanctioning undesirable behavior. Whether these strategies will ultimately prove more successful remains to be seen.

Family Structure Changes

There is far less evidence that choice-based models can explain much of what is observed in family structure patterns. Although theories about welfare effects or the role of male earnings are forcefully argued, existing evidence is quite limited. In the case of welfare, the bulk of evidence to date has shown only small effects. In the case of other economic variables, the research has claimed highly divergent findings. This area ought to be pursued quite actively. It is doubtful, however, that a pure choice framework will ultimately prove as powerful as it seems to be in explaining work and welfare decisions.

But saying that variations in attitudes and expectations are likely to be quite important does not necessarily push one to accept either expectancy or cultural models as these terms have been used here. Those models as presented in this chapter assume that people lack confidence or that they have adverse values. People with confidence and mainstream values can certainly form single-parent households. After all, current research suggests that the typical American child will at some point live in a single-parent home. But some behavior is particularly difficult to reconcile with mainstream values. Births out of wedlock still seem harder to understand and justify than single-parent families caused by separation or divorce. The emphasis on expectations, information, attitudes, culture, and values makes social, psychological, and anthropological models logical candidates for further study.

The expectancy and cultural frameworks seem most helpful in exploring teenage pregnancy. This may be a reflection of the greater quantity of social and psychological research done in this area. But exactly what one is to conclude from this much larger but very diffuse literature is problematic. There seems ample evidence to support almost any model of teenage behavior except a model of pure rational choice. Once again one wonders whether a more complete framework might be developed for thinking about behavior that would make it possible to form a more complete picture of teen pregnancy and sexual behavior. This seems another area in which research that looks at additional factors such as concentration and the effects of various policies would be more enlightening than looking for more evidence of attitudinal or motivational differences.

Although economists are most comfortable with the rational choice model, the other models are thoughtful and intriguing. They provoke a far richer interpretation of welfare and deprivation. Yet they are often quite frustrating as a behavioral construction to be used in research. At times such models seem capable of making widely divergent predictions with only modest variations in assumptions.

Some parts of dependency seem relatively easy to understand with existing paradigms and existing research. Other areas are poorly understood, but research is likely to shed further light on them. Still other areas seem worthy of further attention, but further research may be unlikely to yield a great deal of new insight.

The area that seems to be understood best is the incidence and duration of welfare use among single parents. The patterns observed there seem partially consistent with traditional rational choice paradigms commonly used in policy analysis. When combined with an expectancy model, the behavior looks quite predictable.

But saying that the choice model augmented with some parts of the expectancy framework serves reasonably well does not amount to reporting that such a model gives a clear signal of what might be done to eliminate long-term welfare use. Indeed the models and the empirical results strongly suggest that modest changes in policy will have a relatively small impact on welfare use. In large part this reflects the fact that variations in welfare cannot change the available choices very much. The choice models do offer some hope that nonwelfare supports could make a significant difference. And recent work leads one to wonder what would happen in a system of dramatically changed incentives and supports.

Nor should focusing on such a model suggest that other models themselves do not have very important insights. The idea that self-confidence and the way in which the welfare system treats people may be as important as incentives and choices certainly rings true and deserves much closer scrutiny. Cultural explanations do not seem to explain the bulk of welfare use, but in areas of concentrated poverty such as America's ghettos, they seem to offer insights.

Ghetto poverty seems to deserve special attention and emphasis in future research. The existing evidence indicates that ghetto poverty can only be understood using a combination of all three paradigms. Although such models are likely to be complex and possibly unworkable, there is so much basic information missing about ghetto poverty that research into the area is likely to be quite fruitful.

Existing evidence is probably least helpful in understanding the reasons for family structure changes. None of the paradigms predicts patterns of family structure very well. Although several important hypotheses remain untested, we may not be able to explain these complex changes fully anytime soon. When forces that are hard to understand and measure (such as attitudes and culture) interact with economic and other forces in such a complex manner, it is difficult to discern causality or to devise effective statistical tests. Some promising avenues for research nevertheless remain.

Are the various paradigms useful? The literature offers no definitive explanation for long-term dependency or for why marginal changes in current policy seem to have such modest impacts. Yet all three paradigms offer good clues. As long as work pays so poorly for some women, as long as the only choice is between full-time work with little outside support and welfare, as long as the welfare system provides the only route for some women to get certain benefits such as medical care, and as long as welfare benefits can be collected indefinitely, the rational choice model predicts that many people will become long-term dependents on welfare. As long as welfare is invasive, stigmatizing, isolating, and stifling, expectancy models predict that recipients may "learn helplessness," lacking the confidence and self-esteem necessary to achieve self-support. As long as welfare fails to reflect and reinforce certain traditional values, it will be difficult to promote independence and self-support.

Yet ultimately theoretical constructs have not proved terribly helpful in resolving policy dilemmas with respect to dependency. Thus one of the most important ways to learn is through careful and thoughtful experimentation. And in the end policy will have to be decided on some combination of philosophy and values in combination with hunches and research knowledge.

4

Increasing Self-Sufficiency by Reforming Welfare

America's aspirations for its welfare system have always included eliminating it. In the early nineteenth century, reformers proposed to replace outdoor relief—support for indigents in their own homes—with almshouses or workhouses where the poor would earn their keep and learn to become self-sufficient (Katz 1986). In the 1930s, Social Security was designed to eliminate the need for relief by insuring citizens against the risks of unemployment, old age, and widowhood. In the 1970s and 1980s, reformers with more modest aspirations proposed to reduce the AFDC rolls by establishing employment and training programs.

We continue in the tradition of aspiring to eliminate welfare. Chapter 5 outlines elements of a new system to replace welfare with strategies to make work pay, increase child support, and make welfare transitional. This would be a bold alternative to the current system. History, however, suggests that such large changes are difficult to enact and take even longer to implement effectively. Moreover, important elements of the welfare system, including subsidized employment and training programs, food stamps, and some other forms of both short- and long-term assistance, are likely to be needed even if new nonwelfare programs are put in place. Thus it also makes sense to consider more modest reforms of the welfare system itself, at least for the short run.

Welfare clients and the general public share a frustration with and disdain for the current welfare system. Part of their dissatisfaction stems from the value conflicts inherent in a means-tested, categori-

124

cal system. The difficulties in constructing a means-tested system that is truly compatible with the values of work and family responsibility lead us to advocate nonwelfare strategies as a long-run strategy. Nonetheless, the welfare system could be made much more supportive of the goals of self-sufficiency and work. In addition, client and public contempt for the welfare system develops because the current system operates in ways that are perceived as, and indeed are, arbitrary and unfair. Welfare system reforms need to deal with these irrationalities as well as with issues of self-sufficiency.

Emphasizing Self-Sufficiency

The Family Support Act of 1988 represents an emerging consensus that welfare programs ought to move clients toward self-sufficiency. It attempts to achieve this goal primarily through the requirement that states establish JOBS programs to provide employment and basic skills services, and through a set of transition benefits to ease the financial costs of going to work. AFDC recipients are required to participate in JOBS programs unless they are exempted because they have a child under three or other serious impediments to work.

Whatever other reforms are made in welfare and nonwelfare programs, the means-tested assistance system should embody expectations about and opportunities for moving toward self-sufficiency. The system should also include something like a JOBS program to provide transitional educational, employment, and training services. For both the short and the long term, therefore, it is worth thinking about how the welfare system can reinforce work expectations and about how it can operate employment and training efforts in ways that most effectively promote self-sufficiency.

Reconciling Welfare Administration with the Goal of Self-Sufficiency

From the point of view of clients, welfare involves not just the receipt of a benefits check but a whole system of rules, procedures, and interactions with caseworkers (see Chapter 1). The JOBS program is only a part of what clients encounter. Even more salient to them are interactions regarding eligibility, benefit levels, and the continuation of benefits. These dealings may contradict the intended message of the JOBS program in important ways.

The contradictions come about because of an understandable emphasis in the system on the accuracy of eligibility and benefit level determinations. Welfare is a means-tested system. It is intended for certain types of families with low levels of income from other sources. To fulfill this goal, rules and procedures are needed to determine family status and other income and to adjust benefit levels appropriately. Administering the system well, especially in the context of tight resources and great concern about potential fraud, means making these determinations as accurately as possible.

Yet current administrative practices in the AFDC and Food Stamps programs may lead to increased accuracy at the cost of discouraging self-sufficiency. The bureaucratic requirements for getting and staying on welfare are more difficult and intrusive for people who have nonwelfare sources of income. Federal rules require clients with earned income to provide documentation of amounts earned and the number of hours worked, in the form of wage stubs and letters from employers, on a monthly basis. Failure to submit this information can result in financial penalties, case closings, or delays in receiving benefits. The current system seems to be asking people to prove that they are not working in order to be eligible for assistance; working all too often constitutes welfare "fraud."

During the last decade a well-intentioned federal emphasis on quality control has led states to require periodic redeterminations of eligibility, usually based on mail-in questionnaires or face-to-face recertification interviews. These redeterminations, like the original eligibility interview, are more burdensome for clients with earnings or other outside income. Because clients who have supplemental earned income are considered "error prone," they are often required to appear for face-to-face interviews more frequently than clients who do not work or who do not report the work they do.

Through these requirements, the system seems to be sending the message that it does not expect recipients to work and that it will make their lives more difficult when they do. Such an impression is the exact opposite of what one would like clients to receive—that there are rewards and applause for those who take steps toward self-sufficiency.

A means-tested system must, obviously, collect information about its clients' means, and benefit levels must appropriately reflect available outside income. Nonetheless, reform of both policy and administrative practices to make the operation of the system more consistent with its alleged goals is important. On the administrative side, we need to simplify the eligibility and recertification procedures greatly and place more control and trust in the hands of welfare recipients who are making the effort to work. Welfare administrators should also make a systematic effort to make all aspects of welfare offices' interactions with clients—those concerning eligibility and benefits as well as those explicitly about jobs—supportive of self-sufficiency. To do this mainly involves changes in the behavior and orientation of intake and eligibility workers, who need to see their jobs in the context of an overall mission of promoting self-sufficiency. Case management, in which a worker deals with family problems as a whole and develops a plan for dealing with them, is one approach. Another approach is to design a separate program for recipients who work, into which recipients can "graduate," and in which they are treated more like working people than like welfare recipients. Whether or not eligibility workers become case managers, however, it is important that they as well as JOBS program workers expect and encourage work and efforts toward work.

JOBS Programs

States are at different stages in establishing the Job Opportunity and Basic Skills programs required by the Family Support Act. These new programs need to work well, because they are important components not only of the current system but also of a future system reformed in the ways we suggest later. There are two issues that seem crucial in getting these programs to work well: conveying the appropriate vision of what the programs are about, and measuring progress in appropriate ways. Both are difficult, in part because of the history of previous employment and training programs. In both areas, however, some states have gained useful experience that future efforts can build on.

Conveying the vision: Moving beyond the old debates. Before the passage of the Family Support Act, a number of states had initiated work-related welfare reforms involving various combinations of job search and work obligations with education, employment, and job training services. Some reforms involved "workfare"—recipients working in a public service job to "earn" their welfare benefits—while others explicitly rejected the idea of mandatory work in favor of case management and service packages. The Family Support Act, like some of the state programs before it, reflected a compromise between the supporters and the opponents of mandatory work by requiring participation in the JOBS program but permitting consid-erable flexibility in program activities. It also compromised by em-phasizing work preparation activities over workfare.

As states design and implement the work programs that the Fam-ily Support Act now requires, the tension between traditional pro-ponents and opponents of workfare is likely to continue over the issues of sanctions and over appropriate activities. Much of the debate is ideological, between those who believe that the "right" to welfare ought not to be constrained by work or other requirements and those who believe that welfare receipt carries with it a social obligation to work or prepare for work. Presumably, however, it is also reasonable to ask what kinds of programs are most likely to be successful in moving clients from welfare to self-sufficiency, a goal on which both sides agree. Thinking about the issues that must be dealt with for work-related welfare reform to be successful may provide a way of moving beyond the old debates to a more coherent vision.

Many welfare offices treated the work requirements of the nation-wide Work Incentive program of the 1970s as they treated most other aspects of welfare administration—as paper-processing re-quirements. The welfare worker saw the job as making sure that the client had filled out a work registration form and that the form had been sent to the employment office. The employment worker saw the job as ensuring that the client received a notice to come in, was shown a list of jobs, and filled out a form stating that she was appropriately following up the opportunities that had been presented.

Although the Family Support Act eliminated the requirement for a division of labor between welfare offices and employment services, most states continue to have separate offices and different workers for eligibility determination and employment programs. A referral process must be designed, and there is a continuing danger that it will resemble the old WIN process. This is not a mode of operation likely to lead clients and workers to work hard together to get clients into jobs. What the framers of welfare reform legislation probably had in mind is a style more similar to what Lawrence Mead (1986) described as characterizing successful WIN programs, what Robert Behn (1987, 1991) described in his analyses of the Massachusetts Employment and Training Choices (ET) program, and what MDRC has described in the Riverside County GAIN program.[1]

Mead described the "feel" of effective WIN offices as places where both clients and workers were energetic, working hard, and determined not to get bogged down in paperwork and procedures. "Recipients were constantly coming and going, meeting with the staff, joining training activities, or going out on job interviews. The atmosphere was upbeat. You could feel the electricity just walking into the offices" (Mead 1986, p. 152). Staff were convinced that clients could and should work, and that jobs could be found if only they and the clients put in the effort to find them. Staff worked hard to find jobs for clients and provide the requisite training. They believed and conveyed (and sometimes preached) the idea that work was the norm, and that every client was able and expected to get a job. Neither clients nor workers in high-performing offices, says Mead, were allowed to hide behind the excuses of "no jobs" or "no personal capacity." Workers and clients entered into serious contracts with each other that laid out the responsibility of the worker to provide work opportunities and of the client to work. Workers motivated clients by appeals both to their self-interest (it's better to be working than on welfare) and to their moral sense (we all have obligations to support ourselves and our families).

Behn's description of management innovations in the Massachusetts ET program emphasizes the importance of establishing a clear mission focused on jobs, marketing the program to clients, workers, and the public, convincing both workers and clients that they can achieve the mission, providing the resources to do so, expecting hard work and energy, and monitoring performance. The "feel" of good ET offices—energy, commitment, hard work, trust, confidence that success is possible—seems consistent with other descriptions of well-managed and successful operations. We can be reasonably confident that these characteristics of client and worker interactions are what we ought to be aiming for in work-oriented welfare reform.

The successful Riverside, California, GAIN program has similar features. Management is committed to 100 percent participation, not the lower targets permitted by the Family Support Act. Clients are encouraged to participate in short-term training programs with clear employment potential, rather than less directed, longer-term educational programs. Workers track client attendance and progress, and sanction the minority who are not meeting their obligations. The program is seriously focused on work.

The question is how these successful programs shape an organizational culture that delivers clear messages about goals and expectations, provides resources, and monitors performance. Such a culture must avoid the pitfalls that are inherent in the ways of thinking typically associated with the traditional approaches. Mandatory programs send clear messages that self-sufficiency is serious business and that both workers and clients are expected to perform. They also set up a demand for resources: mandatory programs almost inevitably force the provision of jobs and services, including child care, and in their "workfare" variants, force the creation of jobs. The dangers of mandatory programs lie in their possible tendencies toward nominal compliance, toward adversary relationships between workers and clients in which each blames the other for failures, and toward worker laziness in the form of either blaming or excusing clients.

Voluntary programs, by contrast, can be seen as less serious, and may therefore generate fewer demands for resources. Under good management, however, voluntary programs can engender even more enthusiasm and zeal on the part of both workers and clients than mandatory programs. In voluntary programs, more of the burden of success falls on the workers: they must sell and motivate the clients. In doing so, however, they are likely to convey a strong impression that success is possible, that jobs can be found and that clients can capably fill them. Voluntary programs carry with them a danger that workers will want to deal only with those clients who are easy to serve and will discourage those who are less capable or less motivated. Clients, in turn, may be more willing to let the programs come to them, and if they don't, to lower their own expectations of themselves.

Good programs have been run under either rubric, and bad management can subvert either. If legislators and administrators are seriously committed to achieving successful work programs (and not seeing them simply as a way to deter recipients or cut down the rolls), it does not matter whether the program is mandatory, voluntary, or the FSA compromise of both. What does matter is conveying the vision and paying attention to the difficult issues involved in making programs work. Good management in programs operated under the mandatory rubric appears to require playing down the mandatory aspects in order to motivate workers, circumvent legalistic interpretations of rules, and avoid relying on sanctions as client motivators. Good management in programs operating under a basically voluntary rubric requires playing down the voluntary aspects in order to send clear messages that this is serious business and that both workers and clients are expected to participate and perform.

Family Support Act requirements are consistent with a range of management responses. Federal participation requirements are such that the JOBS program can be operated for only a small proportion of the caseload, with almost all of those who participate doing so on a voluntary basis. A JOBS program can, and in many states does, resemble a small voluntary program. But JOBS programs can also be run with an emphasis on mandatory reporting and sanctioning, with little actual work or employment preparation. Neither approach is likely to be successful. What is necessary is a clear commitment and clear expectations that all clients can and are expected to participate in work or work preparation. Resources and support need to be provided, work experience slots need to be created for those who do not need or want training, and participation needs to be monitored and when necessary sanctioned. Running such a program is neither easy nor cheap, and will run afoul of both budget limitations and political commitments. Nonetheless, only full-scale commitment to serious programs will be successful in changing the image and the reality of welfare.

Changing what counts. A second key element in the effective design and management of work programs is monitoring the performance both of program participants and of the programs themselves.[2] The most common measures for monitoring programs have generally been participation—whether clients participate in some aspect of the program for twenty hours a week or more—and job placements. Participation requirements defined in this way are built into the Family Support Act. Many states use initial job placements as the criterion for judging the success of their programs; this criterion may become part of the federal regulatory process.

For the most disadvantaged clients, however, a more sophisticated approach to defining and monitoring success may be in order. The best analyses of the processes by which very disadvantaged welfare recipients achieve self-sufficiency have been done by Project Match, a work-welfare program that operates in Chicago's Cabrini Green housing project. Project Match has developed the notion of "ladders": steps for clients to move up that are defined by progressively more difficult activities that require gradually increasing time and responsibility commitments. The ladder includes activities with children, volunteer work in the community, and membership in community organizations as well as the more conventional employment, education, and training activities. First steps on the ladder involve time commitments of one to two hours per week, gradually building up to twenty hours per week and then to full-time participation.

The ladder is constructed in such a way that nearly every client is already doing something that can be recorded, praised, and built upon. Project Match works with clients to define next steps, not expecting that everyone will be ready to move into full-time school or work, or that everyone will proceed in the traditional sequence of school followed by work. Instead the expectation is that everyone will do something to make progress toward self-sufficiency. Project workers note each milestone, with ample public recognition for even small steps. They monitor and report whether clients are "on track" and measure their own and their clients' success by whether they are making progress, however slowly or haltingly, up the ladder. They recognize that many clients will fail in their first attempts at school or work, and they define their own responsibility as keeping people trying.

The Project Match ladder is an extremely sensible and creative approach to the issue of accountability in work-welfare programs. Many program operators have opposed performance monitoring, arguing that it encourages "creaming" (concentrating on the clients most likely to succeed) and rewards short-term performance rather than long-term achievement. But the accountability/discretion argument, like the mandatory/voluntary argument, is one that work programs need to move beyond. Programs *must* be accountable, and must have some way of knowing and showing others whether they are doing a good job. They will have to count, and so the trick will be to count what really counts. A tool like the Project Match ladder can be an important contribution to both program management and accountability.

Restoring Rationality and Fairness

For the welfare system to be morally legitimate in the eyes of its clients and the taxpayers, it needs to embody not only the values of self-sufficiency and responsibility but also the values of fairness and rationality. Both clients and taxpayers have the right to expect the system to treat people equitably and humanely and to allow them information about and some control over their fate. These qualities are lacking in many aspects of the current system.

An Irrational and Mysterious System

The current welfare system is the historical product of competing tendencies in program design and administration (see Chapter 1).

The original AFDC legislation set up a federal-state partnership that gave the federal government authority over the basic regulatory structure and the states jurisdiction over benefit levels and administration. Reforms of the AFDC system in the 1960s emphasized participation, client rights, and the separation of income support from what were seen as overly intrusive social services. Welfare reforms of the 1970s and 1980s emphasized tighter control of eligibility and spending and the reintroduction of services, especially those related to employment. In addition, the Food Stamps, Medicaid, and housing assistance programs developed their own regulatory structures. The legacy of these competing reforms is a system that is enormously rule-bound and complex and that contains a fair number of internal contradictions.[3]

Means-tested programs inevitably need rules and procedures for determining income, establishing "needs," and setting benefit levels. As part of their quality control programs in AFDC and Medicaid, many states established standard rules and procedures for determining eligibility and uniform benefit levels. The federal government standardized rules and procedures for food stamps and housing assistance. The new system is rational, discretion-proof, and auditable. It is not, however, transparent to clients, workers, or the public. AFDC eligibility and benefit levels vary by household size and composition, and also vary between states and in some states between counties. Some kinds of income and resources are counted for purposes of eligibility determination while others are not; and various deductions and exemptions, for items such as work expenses, are made from income before it is counted.

To make matters worse, public assistance programs seem to change continuously and to become ever more complicated. Rules are different for AFDC, Food Stamps, Medicaid, and housing assistance; both the Congress and individual state legislatures change them frequently. Legal challenges frequently result in further modification of the rules, sometimes for the nation as a whole and sometimes only for particular jurisdictions. State central office bureaucrats can often barely keep up with translating legislative changes and judicial decisions into forms and procedures that workers can use, not to mention explaining to workers or clients the logic or lack thereof behind the changes.

In recent years, eligibility rules and benefit levels have become even more of a "black box" to clients and workers. Part of this has to do with changes in the work environment of welfare offices. When welfare became more rule-bound and less discretionary, workers changed from being general caseworkers who assessed needs and provided services to being "examiners" who collected information and applied rules. Application forms, interview guides, and budget workbooks were designed for workers with high school educations and little training. Training and supervision of workers focused on procedures. It was no longer necessary for workers to get to know clients beyond the information required by procedures.

At the same time, most states installed computer systems that automatically determined eligibility and calculated benefit levels based on the information collected by examiners and entered into the machines by data entry personnel. Because workers are not responsible for calculating budgets, they have no need to understand how the information they are collecting affects eligibility or benefits. Needless to say, clients are not likely to understand the process or to feel that they have much control over their fates. Some thirty days after they apply, clients receive in the mail a notice designed by lawyers that informs them that they either have or have not been determined eligible and what their benefits will be.

The result of all this is that the welfare system has become more and more mysterious and apparently arbitrary to workers and clients. Genuine bewilderment may explain some of the helplessness and frustration that clients at times display as they confront the welfare system. Some of the apparent irrationality that researchers find in the lack of response to program incentives or disincentives may be explainable. If people have no real idea how their benefit levels are determined, they probably do not know whether a $1.00 increase in earnings will change their benefit levels by nothing, everything, or something in between. If they do not know or understand the circumstances in which Medicaid or child-care assistance would or would not be continued after they leave welfare, they cannot fully understand the implications of attempting to go to work. Moreover, if their benefits are discontinued or reduced for apparently arbitrary reasons, as happens to at least some clients every time the rules change, they may lose confidence that they can control their own destinies. A lack of clear understanding about the program seems likely to affect clients' choices about work and welfare, and to influence the sense of control they have over their own lives.

The reforms that follow from this analysis are basically simple, but very important. We should minimize program changes, except for those changes that make the system simpler and easier to understand. We should move toward a common definition of a filing unit and income eligibility levels for the major assistance programs. Serious efforts should be made to communicate clearly and effectively with welfare recipients about the programs and their own participation in them. Workers should be trained and expected to understand their programs and to understand that part of their jobs should be helping clients understand and control the program and their lives. Within this framework, simplification is not just a matter of administrative neatness and efficiency (computers make neatness less important). It is instead an extremely important reform in terms of the messages that the system sends its clients about rationality, fairness, and control.

Irrational Benefit Structures

Another contributor to perceptions that the welfare system is irrational and unfair is the structure of welfare benefits. AFDC benefit levels are set by the states, and vary quite dramatically, with maximums ranging in 1992 from $120 per month for a family of three in Mississippi to $680 per month in Connecticut; the median state paid $372. Nearly all AFDC families also receive food stamps, which in 1992 supplemented benefits in the amounts of $184–$292 per month and equalized the distribution somewhat. Combined AFDC and Food Stamps benefits provide income levels that range from about 46 percent of the poverty line in Mississippi to about 95 percent in Vermont and Connecticut; in the median state combined

AFDC and Food Stamps benefits amount to about 72 percent of the poverty line (U.S. House, Ways and Means 1992, pp. 636–637). About a quarter of welfare recipients also receive housing benefits, either by living in public housing or by participating in a housing assistance program. Housing assistance provides benefits equal to the difference between rent costs and one third of the recipient's income up to a maximum fair market rent for the area. Recipients cannot legally supplement benefits with either work or child support. The presumed expectation is that families live within these benefit levels.

One way to get a sense of what these benefit levels mean to the families that must live on them and of how much variation there is among recipients is to estimate income and spending for welfare recipients with no other income. Food stamp benefit levels are based on an economy food budget that is meant to provide a nutritious but basic diet; the cost of that diet in 1992 was estimated at $292 per month for a family of three (U.S. House, Ways and Means 1992, p. 1624). Data on the cost of rental housing is collected and published by HUD. Its estimates of fair market rents for a two-bedroom unit range from $350 to $400 per month for many cities in the South to over $600 per month in the urban areas of Washington, D.C., Massachusetts, New York, and a few others (U.S. HUD 1991).

These estimates can be used to compare income with estimated necessary spending for food and rent, and to calculate "discretionary income" available for spending on utilities, household expenses, clothing, transportation, and other living costs. Table 4.1 shows estimates for California, Illinois, and Texas, for recipients who receive housing assistance and those who do not.[4] Total income varies considerably among the states. Even more dramatic, however, is the variation in "discretionary income," which ranges from an estimated $301 per month for a housing assistance recipient in California to an estimated *negative* $192 per month for a recipient in Texas who does not receive housing assistance. It is worth noting that California is an outlier in terms of discretionary income; levels of discretionary income in Illinois are much more typical. Recipients who pay market rents for housing will have *negative* discretionary income in thirty-eight states and less than $30 a month in six more.

Table 4.1 Income and spending for AFDC recipients, selected states, 1991

| | California | | | | | |
| | Assisted housing | | | Not assisted housing | | |
Expense category	Food stamps	AFDC	Spending	Food stamps	AFDC	Spending
Food	129	163	292	187	105	292
Housing		199	199		453	453
Other		301	301		105	105
Total	129	663	792	187	663	850

| | Illinois | | | | | |
| | Assisted housing | | | Not assisted housing | | |
	Food stamps	AFDC	Spending	Food stamps	AFDC	Spending
Food	218	74	292	282	10	292
Housing		110	110		357	464
Other		183	183			−107
Total	218	367	585	282	367	649

| | Texas | | | | | |
| | Assisted housing | | | Not assisted housing | | |
	Food stamps	AFDC	Spending	Food stamps	AFDC	Spending
Food	273	19	292	292		292
Housing		55	55		184	376
Other		110	110			−192
Total	273	184	457	292	184	476

AFDC rules are such that working or receiving child support reduces benefits almost dollar for dollar after work expenses. A woman who worked half-time at $4.25 an hour and who followed the rules could increase her disposable income in the median state by about $100 a month, almost enough to make up her rent in a state like Illinois but not enough to provide more than a bit of discretionary income. A woman who worked full-time at $4.25 an hour or half-time at $8.00 an hour would increase her discretionary income by about the same amount. She cannot legally do better than this, no matter what she receives from work or child support, short of getting the full-time good-wage job that would allow her to get off welfare entirely. For the lucky quarter or so who receive housing assistance, of course, it is possible to do better than this.

Christopher Jencks and Kathryn Edin (1990) interviewed a sample of twenty-five welfare recipients in a midwestern city to find out how they lived on combined welfare/food stamps benefit levels that were below the basic costs of food and rent. Their respondents lived dreary and difficult lives, in unsafe neighborhoods and poor housing, with basic diets and few non-necessities. Even so, however, they did not live on their welfare checks alone. All of the respondents supplemented their income, on average doubling it, through a combination of illegitimate income and legitimate earnings that they did not report to the welfare department. Jencks and Edin interpret this as understandable and indeed moral behavior, even though their respondents were violating the rules of the system. They argue that, for the clients, perceived obligations to support one's family override perceived obligations to obey the rules of a system that makes it impossible to support the family. Moreover, they argue, a system in which one cannot improve one's lot by working is not perceived as a legitimate system. Clients believe that when they work they ought to be better off, and so they keep their earnings without reporting them. They ignore rules that they perceive as violating important norms. Jencks and Edin argue that such a system undercuts moral legitimacy, reinforcing, again, a perceived inability to make it while playing by the rules.

Laura Lein (1989, 1991), who has conducted similar research in a southwestern city, reports even more depressing findings. She focused on how families attempting to live on extremely low welfare benefits managed to feed themselves. She did not find widespread income supplementation, perhaps because work opportunities were so limited in the area in which she was working. Instead she found families spending enormous amounts of time and energy taking advantage of food pantries, school and camp feeding programs, and so on. They too "cheated": lying to the soup kitchens about whether they received food stamps; relying on their children to smuggle home food for the family from the day camp lunch program. Lein also found evidence of reasonably widespread low-level malnutrition. She too argues that the system has lost moral legitimacy, forcing its recipients to violate program rules to achieve the higher (for them and for her) moral goal of feeding their families.

Proposals to raise benefit levels tend to generate little enthusiasm among policymakers. At least two large states have instead recently cut their benefit levels even in nominal terms; many more states have cut them in real terms by not increasing them with inflation. Even Jencks and Edin conclude that raising benefits would be a mistake, arguing instead for guaranteed child support and work programs.

Proponents of work and child support tend to ignore the issue of welfare benefit levels, assuming that child support plus work plus an expanded Earned Income Tax Credit (EITC) plus, presumably, food stamps will make the need for adequate welfare benefits disappear. But there are a number of circumstances under which this will not be true. Many women on welfare, at least in the beginning, are not in a position to earn enough per month to raise their incomes above the poverty line. Clients without work experience and skills will need at least transitional benefits. Some women will be unable to obtain child support orders. And women with infants are unlikely to be able to work, at least without substantial and expensive support.

Several alternative approaches can be considered. The least radical would be for the federal government to require states to establish, regularly update, and publish state standards of need, based on food stamp levels for food, market rents for housing, and reasonable allowances for energy, transportation, clothing, and so on. States could then set their own benefit levels, which might be below these standards of need, but they would be left to explain how they expected welfare recipients to support their families.

This kind of consistent listing of needs and benefits might well discourage benefit level cuts and perhaps lead to benefit level increases in low-benefit states. An alternative approach now being tried by many states is to increase the types and amounts of income that are disregarded in calculating AFDC benefits, on the assumption that families need and are mostly able to get income from other sources. Some states disregard all or part of families' income from the EITC, from child support, and from earnings. Doing this has the effect of increasing benefits for families that receive income from these other sources.

A more radical approach would be to transform the welfare system into a set of consumption subsidies and time-limited special allowances. Such a proposal might keep the Food Stamps program in its current form, and combine AFDC and the housing assistance programs into a coherent housing assistance program. Recipients in the housing assistance program might get benefits sufficient to cover some fraction of fair market rent plus reasonable utility costs in their area; they would be expected to contribute a reasonable fraction of their income. To supplement consumption subsidies states might provide special allowances on a transitional basis for special categories of people—for example, recipients in training programs or those caring for infants.

A consumption-based scheme of this sort could be easily integrated with the reforms proposed in Chapter 5. It would speak to the public resentment of welfare recipients who appear to have, and in some cases do have, more discretionary income than working families. At the same time, it would increase the real and perceived legitimacy of the system in two ways. First, it would embody an expectation that people had outside sources of income that were theirs, but that they were expected to spend mostly on basic necessities. Second, it would allow welfare recipients to provide basic necessities to their families and to support them at a slightly higher level if they had earnings or other outside income. It would thus provide a genuine opportunity for recipients to support their families without breaking the rules of the system. This alternative may be worth considering along with more conventional approaches.

Reforming Welfare Reform

Some means-tested assistance programs are likely to be with us for a long time. Even under the most optimistic scenarios, programs such as Food Stamps, housing assistance, transitional employment and training, and perhaps special allowance for infant care will be necessary, especially for families with very young children. Reforming welfare to restore moral legitimacy and to promote self-sufficiency is consistent with the goals of the broader reforms. Serious reforms could also bring about substantial improvements over the current system in the event that the more radical replacements for welfare are some time in coming.

The important reforms involve both policy and management. One very important policy reform is to simplify the system and make it understandable to workers and clients. It is also important to restructure benefits and incentives in order to restore moral legitimacy to the system. The management reforms are perhaps even more significant. They are meant to transform the mission of the welfare program to focus on self-sufficiency and to have that mission reflected in total program operations. All the reforms ought to embody respect and high expectations for clients, assuming that even long-term welfare recipients can exercise control over their destinies and make progress toward independent mainstream lives.

Like reformers in the nineteenth century, the 1930s, and more recently, we would much prefer to live in a society in which means-tested welfare was a trivial component of income support policies. In the short run, however, it is important to make it the best program we can.

5

Reducing Poverty by Replacing Welfare

For at least twenty years, the rhetoric of poverty policy has focused on work and family and independence. Yet the reality of poverty policy has been welfare. And welfare does almost nothing to promote work or family or independence. Welfare almost never *solves* problems; it *salves* them with dollars.

Welfare needs to be replaced, not reformed with a few new programs and requirements, not eliminated leaving poor people with little or no support or protection, but replaced. It needs to be replaced with policies that treat the causes of poverty. It needs to be replaced with a system of income support that reinforces principles of work and family and independence.

Three principles must be adopted if we are truly to replace the welfare system.

- People who work shouldn't be poor. Those who are playing by the rules should not lose the game.

- One parent should not be expected to do the job of two. In a single-parent family, children need support from both parents.

- Government aid ought to be designed to encourage and support work and independence. Long-term income-tested cash support for those who can work ought to be avoided. We ought to do more to help people help themselves, and we ought to expect more in return.

143

Adoption of these principles would do far more to help our poor children than fifty years of welfare policy. Ignoring them dooms almost any poverty policy to failure.

American Poverty, American Policy

Americans misunderstand the nature of poverty. Less than 10 percent of poor children live in big-city ghetto neighborhoods. At least twice that number live in two-parent families with a full-time worker. The feminization of poverty is real. But single-parent poverty is not confined to people of color. As already noted, the typical child born in America today will spend time living in a single-parent home. And the poverty rate in single-parent families with children is nearly 50 percent.

Americans deeply distrust, even despise, welfare, our chief social policy to help poor families. Liberals decry the very low benefits. Conservatives argue that it breeds dependency and illegitimacy. The recipients often hate it most of all, claiming that it leaves them isolated, frustrated, and humiliated. No one believes that welfare solves problems. At best it tides people over until they can get back on their feet. At worst it creates a dead end, a world offering few routes to independence, and little dignity or self-respect.

With the media filled with stereotypical and racially charged images of the ghetto poor and with welfare debates a staple of angry talk shows, it is no wonder that the public is skeptical, even cynical, about the nation's capacity to help the poor. But poverty is much easier to understand than many people realize. And practical and affordable nonwelfare solutions *do* exist.

People Who Work Shouldn't Be Poor

People who work can be poor in America. Over five million poor people live in families with a full-year full-time worker. Several times that number live in families in which someone works part of the year. And many more live in families on welfare in circumstances where full-time work would leave the family poor and financially no better off than on welfare. The reality is that for millions of Americans, work simply does not pay.

Depending on the state of the economy, between 40 and 50 percent of the poor children in America live in two-parent homes. These are working families. Table 5.1, which is based on tabulations of the March 1988 Current Population Survey (the survey used for official poverty statistics), shows that only 9 percent of poor two-parent families had two healthy and nonelderly parents who did not work at all. Almost 44 percent (40.9 percent plus 2.9 percent) of poor two-parent families had a full-year full-time worker, and well over half of the poor families with two healthy parents had at least one full-time worker. Work is very much the norm for these families. Notice also that in most families with only a part-year worker, that worker earned too little to get the family out of poverty even if the job had lasted all year.

It may seem remarkable that so many people are able to work without being able to support a family. Of course, the overwhelming majority (over 90 percent) of two-parent families with one or more full-time workers do avoid poverty. But work is no guarantee of success for those at the lower end of the wage spectrum. A full-time job paying $3.35 per hour (the minimum wage from 1981 to 1990) cannot support even two persons above the current poverty line. As shown in Table 5.2, by 1992, when the minimum wage had been raised to $4.25 per hour, one full-time minimum wage job left a family of four more than $5,000 below the poverty line. (One full-time and one part-time job would still leave a family of four $1,500 per year below the poverty line of $14,500, even if they had *no* day-care expenses.)

These families are working hard at some of the most unpleasant jobs in America. They ride the same economic roller coaster as the rest of us. When real wages for the middle class rise rapidly, as they did in the 1960s, the wages of working poor families rise as well. A strong economy is very good medicine. But wages have been essentially stagnant for twenty years after adjusting for inflation. The median real income for all full-time male workers in America is lower today than in 1969. For the first time in many generations, sons are earning less than their fathers did.

Table 5.1 Distribution of poor husband-wife families by health, work status, and wage rate relative to the poverty line

Health, work status, wage	Distribution of poor families (%)
Neither parent ill, disabled, or retired and:	
At least one parent worked full-time full year	40.9
Combined work of both parents was equal to at least one full-year full-time worker	3.1
One or both parents worked, but combined hours were less than one full-year full-time worker and:	
—Wage was NOT high enough to keep family out of poverty if a person worked at the job full-time all year[a]	20.3
—Wage was high enough to keep family out of poverty if a person worked full-time all year[a]	4.9
Neither parent worked	9.0
One or both parents ill, disabled, or retired and:	
Other parent worked full-time full year	2.9
Other parent worked some, but less than full-time, full year	6.9
Neither parent worked	12.1
Total	100.0

Source: Authors' tabulations of the March 1988 Current Population Survey.
Note: Full-year full-time work is defined as 1,759 hours of work annually.
a. Computed by determining the average wage by dividing annual earnings by total hours, and multiplying this average wage by 1,750 to get an estimate of potential annual earnings, and comparing this with the poverty line for the family.

Table 5.2 Earnings and income for a family with one full-year full-time
worker in 1992[a]

	Hourly wage		
	$4.25	$5.50	$7.00
Earnings	$8,500	$11,000	$14,000
Social Security	−650	−842	−1,071
EITC	1,384	1,384	1,100
Disposable income—no day-care costs	$9,234	$11,543	$14,029
Disposable income with $2,000 day-care costs	$7,234	$ 9,543	$12,029

Note: Poverty line in 1992 was $11,300 for a family of three and $14,500 for a family
of four.

a. Assumes EITC phase in = .184; phase out = .1314; phase out starts at $11,840;
Social Security tax rate = .0765. All figures are approximate.

And when the economy stumbles, the working poor fall. They
have disproportionately borne the brunt of economic changes of the
past few decades. There is now clear evidence that the workers at
the upper end of the economic distribution have fared far better
over the recent past than those at the bottom. Young workers, the
less well educated, and people of color were hurt more by the
recession and helped less by the recovery.

What do we currently do to support these families? Virtually
nothing. They do not qualify for public assistance other than food
stamps, and many are too proud to apply for stamps. They get
almost no government medical benefits, which go mostly to welfare
recipients. After government transfers, poor two-parent families
with a full-time worker have incomes farther below the poverty line
than single-parent families on welfare or two-parent families with
an unemployed worker. The working poor are literally the poorest
of the poor.

And low pay is not simply a problem for two-parent families. The
nature of our welfare system is such that unless a single mother can

find a full-time job that pays at least $5 or $6 or $7 an hour with medical benefits, along with very inexpensive day care, she will be better off on welfare.

Unless we find a way to make work pay, we can never make much progress in the fight against the poverty of children. And unless we find a way to make work pay, millions of children will grow up seeing that hard work doesn't pay off, that work is not an alternative to welfare. They will discover that you can play by the rules and still lose the game.

Make Work Pay

If we are going to make work pay, two types of measures must be adopted:

1. We must use a combination of wage and tax policies to ensure that a full-time worker earns enough to keep his or her family out of poverty (including the cost of day care).

2. We must ensure that medical protection is available to all low-income families, not just those on welfare.

This section focuses primarily on the first item. In thinking about the second, however, we must remember that every other major industrialized country except South Africa has found a way to ensure that all its citizens have medical protection. And they spend far less on health care than this country does now. Medical emergencies can easily destroy everything a low-income family has worked for. And we usually end up paying the bills later anyway, in the form of higher health insurance costs that are used to cover the bad debts of hospitals.

How can we ensure that people who work will not be poor? There are two major types of policies: wage policies, such as raising the minimum wage, and refundable tax credits, such as the Earned Income Tax Credit. The proposals here are in 1992 dollars.

Throughout the late 1950s, 1960s, and 1970s, the minimum wage was kept at a level that would enable a full-time worker to keep a family of three out of poverty. But during the 1980s, the minimum was not adjusted with inflation and its real value fell sharply. If the minimum wage were restored to the level it stood at during the 1960s and 1970s (a level sufficient to keep a family of three out of poverty), it would have had to rise to roughly $5.50 per hour in 1992. Recent legislation raised it to $4.25 in 1991, still lower than in 1956, adjusting for inflation.

But a higher minimum wage has costs. All economists agree that there will be some job losses among teenagers. And the vast majority of people in minimum wage jobs are not in poor families. Most estimates suggest that working poor families would be helped by a higher minimum wage, but that there will be economic costs.

An alternative policy is a higher EITC. We already have a tax credit for low-income working families, and recent legislation has expanded it. Because it is refundable, poor families get the credit even if they owe no taxes. In 1990 the plan provided families with a $.14 credit for each dollar earned up to $6,800, for a maximum of $953. The credit is phased out with a $.10 reduction for each dollar earned over $10,740. It is like a pay raise for the working poor. The 1990 EITC was worth about $.50 per hour. The credit was large enough to roughly offset Social Security taxes paid by low-income workers.

Because the EITC imposes no costs on employers, there are no job losses. Because it is done through the tax system, credits can be targeted to poor and near-poor families. Indeed, expanding the EITC was so attractive that academics from the far left to the far right endorsed it, resulting in legislation in the fall of 1990. When phased in by 1994, for families with one child, the credit would rise to $.23 of each dollar earned up to $8,090, for a maximum of $1,861. Families with more children or a child under one would receive somewhat more. Families with out-of-pocket health insurance costs also got a supplemental benefit.

This expansion was a major policy change, the single largest expansion of benefits for low-income families in decades. But it did not go far enough. It still did not ensure that working families would avoid poverty. What would it take to ensure that a full-time minimum wage worker could support a family of four sufficiently to keep it out of poverty in 1992? Table 5.3 illustrates the choices. The 1992 EITC would leave a family of four with a full-time full-year minimum wage worker over $5,000 below the poverty level (if the family did not collect food stamps). Even tripling the EITC above its 1992 level would leave the family $2,500 short. If the family must pay for day care, then even more income would be needed to avoid poverty.

Achieving this goal probably requires a combination of policies. If one tripled the EITC of 1992 and raised the minimum wage to $5.50, the goal would essentially be achieved. Conversely, if one accepts having poor working families collect food stamps (as the law allows), then a combination of tripling the EITC of 1992 and food stamps keeps a minimum wage family of four out of poverty. But many poor working families do not want to collect food stamps, and ideally one would prefer that such families avoid getting into the welfare jumble. Without food stamp benefits, the only practical way of ensuring that working families avoid poverty is both to expand the EITC and to raise the minimum wage. Help with the expenses of child care is also essential. If we believe that people who play by the rules should not lose the game, we must use a combination of policies to make work pay.

(After this chapter was completed, a significantly expanded EITC was proposed by President Clinton and passed by the Congress. The new EITC is close to the level shown as triple the 1992 EITC in Table 5.3.)

Policies to help the working poor reinforce work. They reward people for their efforts. They help two-parent working families. They encourage independence. They do not lead to dependency.

One Parent Shouldn't Be Expected to Do the Job of Two

Making work pay and guaranteeing medical protection would help many poor children a great deal, especially those in two-parent families. Children in single-parent families would be helped also. Low pay is a particularly serious problem for single parents. The job market still pays women far less than men.

But there are two other problems that single parents face that these policies do not address: their dual role as both nurturer and provider and a hostile welfare system. All parents, married or single, face a difficult task of nurturing and providing for their children.

Table 5.3 Disposable income for family of four with one full-year full-time worker, under 1992 law and various proposals[a]

	Hourly wage		
	$4.25	$5.50	$7.00
Family with no food stamps			
EITC as of 1992	$ 9,234	$11,543	$14,029
Double 1992 EITC	10,618	12,927	15,129
Triple 1992 EITC	12,002	14,311	16,230
Family with food stamps			
EITC as of 1992	12,461	14,170	16,004
Double 1992 EITC	13,513	15,221	16,840
Triple 1992 EITC	14,564	16,273	17,677

Note: Poverty line in 1992 was $11,300 for a family of three and $14,500 for a family of four.

a. Assumes EITC phase in = .184; phase out = .1314; phase out starts at $11,840; Social Security tax rate = .0765. All figures are approximate.

Two-parent families can balance those duties in a variety of ways. Indeed the most common arrangement today is for both parents to work. But usually only the father works full-time all year. The mother usually works part-time or part-year. Only 30 percent of married mothers work full-year full-time. But single parents don't have that kind of flexibility. They really only have two choices: they can either work all the time or they can go on welfare.

If single parents choose full-time work, they must simultaneously meet the demands of work and the need for child care, the many daily crises involving doctor visits, school holidays, sick children, to say nothing of maintaining a safe and happy household. Women from highly advantaged backgrounds find these demands very heavy. For mothers with a limited education, with little or no work experience, with young children, it can be an almost impossible task. Is it really realistic (or fair) to expect all single mothers to work more than 70 percent of married mothers do?

The only alternative at present is welfare. And it is not a very attractive option. No state pays enough in welfare and food stamps to keep a family out of poverty. Adjusting for inflation, benefits are vastly lower than they were fifteen years ago. The welfare system frustrates, isolates, humiliates, and stigmatizes. Welfare offices are designed in large part to prevent fraud and abuse, to deliver aid in the right amount at the right time. Applying for welfare is a major undertaking. A variety of verifications must be done. Inevitably, welfare clients must return repeatedly to the welfare office. Welfare and food stamps and housing and social services are separate programs, each with its own rules, its own demands, and sometimes its own office.

Worse still is the way welfare treats people who try to play by the rules, people who attempt to work their way off of welfare. Welfare benefits are reduced dollar for dollar with earnings. Table 5.4 shows that a woman working full-time at $4.25, the 1992 minimum wage, is not much better off than someone who does no work at all. Even a woman with very low day-care costs who can earn $6.00 per hour may be not much better off working. She will take home only about $3,000 more per year and she will lose Medicaid benefits which are worth almost that amount. How many disadvantaged women can find and retain a full-time job that pays such a premium over the minimum wage?

It should come as no surprise that only a minority (about 40 percent) of women leaving welfare actually "earn" their way off. And most of them are the better educated and more experienced women who can command a relatively high wage. Other women try to leave, but there is almost always some setback, often something relatively small, such as a sick child, which causes them to lose their job and return to welfare. No wonder the most common way to leave welfare permanently is via marriage, not work.

We would like single parents to support themselves and become self-sufficient, but we have made the task almost impossible. Welfare reform begins the process of moving the government toward a system that encourages and facilitates self-support rather than seeming to defeat it. But it doesn't alter the basic dilemmas inherent in a welfare system. It doesn't make work pay. It doesn't make it

Table 5.4 Earnings, taxes, benefits, and total income for a single parent and two children living in Pennsylvania, 1991

Work level and wage	Earnings	Day care	Taxes[a]	EITC	Welfare and food stamps	Disposable income[b]	Medicaid?
No work	$0	$0	$0	$0	$7,278	$7,278	Yes
Half-time, minimum wage[c]	$4,250	−1,500	−325	735	5,185	8,345	Yes
Full-time, minimum wage[c]	$8,500	−3,000	−650	1,235	1,989	8,074	Yes
Full-time, $5.00 per hour	$10,000	−3,000	−555	1,235	1,719	9,399	No
Full-time, $6.00 per hour	$12,000	−3,000	−886	1,143	1,376	10,633	No
Full-time, $7.00 per hour	$14,000	−3,000	−1,309	895	1,060	11,647	No

Note: All figures are approximate. Modeled after a table in U.S. House, Ways and Means (1992).

a. Taxes include Social Security, federal, and state taxes.

b. Earnings plus EITC, AFDC, and food stamps less taxes and day care.

c. Minimum wage rate is $4.25 per hour.

possible to support a family on anything less than a full-time job that pays almost twice the minimum wage along with medical benefits. It doesn't ensure that a woman is better off working than on welfare.

The reason single parents have such a difficult time is that we are expecting one parent to do the job of two. Without some additional support, all single parents face a difficult struggle. Single mothers with weak educations and limited work experience are virtually assured of being stuck in the welfare system.

Insured Child Support Enforcement: A Real Welfare Alternative

Single parents must get some additional, nonwelfare support if there is any realistic hope of escaping welfare. Because it is a lack of support from two parents that is a large part of the problem, the absent father is the natural place to look for additional income.

The current system of child support is a disgrace. Only one single parent in three gets any court-ordered child support from the absent parent, and the average amount is only $2,200. Often the problem is not that the father cannot pay. By most estimates a truly uniform and universal child support system could collect an additional $20–$30 billion from fathers. Remember, this problem is not limited to children in ghetto communities. The typical child born in America today will spend time in a single-parent home. The current system essentially lets fathers off the hook. We are sending the signal to parents and children that absent fathers have no responsibilities.

Suppose a woman could count on just $2,000 per child in child support annually. Then a combination of work and child support could easily support a family at the poverty line. Even half-time work at a job paying $6 per hour would be enough to keep a family of three out of poverty in 1992. Full-time work would provide some real security.

An insured child support enforcement plan could combine tough yet reasonable child support enforcement with a guaranteed benefit. Absent parents would be held accountable. But when collections from the absent father fell below some minimum level (because of low earnings of the father), the government would make up the difference. The plan would include four elements:

1. Both parents' Social Security numbers would be identified at birth or, for those children who are born abroad, upon application to the system.

2. Child support payments would be determined by a very simple formula. The Wisconsin formula, for example, requires the absent parent to pay 17 percent for one child, 24 percent for two, and so forth.

3. All payments would be collected like taxes by the state through automatic wage withholding by the employer. All child support payments would be collected in this way, so all women would be in the same system.

4. The government would ensure that each child received at least $2,000 per year in child support if a child support order were in place. When collections from the absent parent fell below that level, the government would make up the difference.

The first three elements of the plan are not controversial. They have already been adopted as part of the Family Support Act (though with little real incentive to enforce them). The real stumbling block will be the fourth element—the insured benefit.

Some argue that a minimum child support benefit is simply welfare by another name. I strongly disagree. When a woman earns an extra dollar while on welfare, benefits are reduced by a dollar. When she earns an extra dollar while collecting child support, she keeps the whole dollar. Child support will not require trips to the welfare office. There will be no stigma, no reporting, no verification, and no cheating. Moreover, if the public starts complaining about the money being spent on insured child support benefits, they will say, "Those darn *fathers* are not pulling their weight; we are paying their child support for them!" And there will be fights about workfare for fathers versus training and education. The struggles and responsibilities of fathers will be debated as part of our concern for the single-parent families, just as they should be. And perhaps most important, the same uniform system will protect working-class, and middle-class, and upper-class families.

Such a system should ideally be part of the Social Security system. The greatest source of insecurity in America used to be growing old. We dramatically reduced that problem with Social Security, which covers all American families, where contributions and benefits are related to earnings, but where people at the bottom had extra protection. A uniform child support insurance plan would do the same. Contributions would be collected from all absent parents, and that money would go directly to the children. And there would be extra protection for those at the bottom.

The most remarkable feature of the system is that it will not cost very much. Most of the payments come from the absent fathers. For women on welfare the minimum benefits will simply offset welfare payments and thus cost nothing extra. The only real cost is for people who are off welfare, achieving independence by combining work and child support. Most estimates suggest that the cost will be small. And if additional money is spent, it will all be going to women who are working—families who are playing by the rules and trying to provide for themselves. Thus the system will reinforce work and family and parental responsibility.

With such a system, single mothers would for the first time have some money they could count on: money to supplement their own earnings; money to help them meet the "minor" crises that often force people back on welfare; money to make it possible to achieve real independence from welfare; money to get out of poverty. Without such a system, poverty rates for single parents will always be astronomical.

Transitional Support and Jobs

Welfare suffers from schizophrenia. Is welfare a program to ensure the long-term protection of children or is it a program to help people temporarily in times of trouble? Should welfare benefits be raised to reduce the poverty of those getting benefits or lowered to encourage their independence? A program of long-term income support would probably be designed very differently from one designed to offer transitional assistance. By trying to fill both roles, the current system has done neither very well.

In the last round of welfare reform, some of the uncertainty seemed to vanish. All sides settled on a conception of welfare as transitional. The primary objective was to help people over a period of hardship and achieve some real independence. But because little was done to ensure that work pays or to guarantee that single parents could count on some child support, there is little hope that the reformed welfare system will be truly transitional.

But if we had an effective child support enforcement and insurance system, if we ensured that people got medical protection, if we made work pay, there would be far less need for welfare. Single parents could realistically support themselves at the poverty line if they were willing to work half time, even at a job paying little more than the minimum wage. If they were willing to work full time, they could move well above the poverty line. Two-parent families could avoid poverty with a single full-time worker or two half-time workers.

With this kind of support in place, one could more easily contemplate major changes in welfare. There is clear evidence that many single parents have short-term transitional problems. A divorce or separation or birth of a child takes time for adjustment. Often women spend a few years on welfare before remarrying or going to work. Indeed half of the women who go on AFDC have spells lasting two years or less. The last thing new single mothers need is immediate stress. They need help and support. If a woman has never worked before, it will not be easy to move right into a new job. If she has young children, it may be undesirable and impractical to expect her to work right away. And economic fluctuations will inevitably create short-term problems for both single-parent and two-parent families. Thus transitional assistance would be necessary.

If people can realistically support themselves, then the notion of a time-limited, transitional assistance program for both single-parent and two-parent families makes sense. A rich set of training and support services ought to be included as part of the benefits. But the cash benefit program would be of limited duration. There would be no confusion of the point of the program for beneficiaries, administrators, or the public. It would be designed to help people achieve independence. In the case of single mothers, with child support and measures to make work pay, the realistic goal would be to get mothers part-time or full-time work.

The duration of assistance might be allowed to vary with the age of the youngest child. Generally it might last eighteen months to three years, depending on how old the youngest child is. But the key is that this assistance would be *transitional*. One could not re-qualify for much more transitional assistance by having another baby or by claiming that no jobs were available. The transitional program would be society's attempt to offer short-term aid and an opportunity for support and training. It would reflect the clear recognition that people often need help over a difficult period.

When benefits were used up, one would have to work for some period to requalify for more. Many support services—certainly child care and some training—might continue past the transitional period, but cash benefits would end. After benefits ran out, the only alternative for support would be to supplement child support with work.

There are a number of concerns which must be addressed if we are to move to a truly transitional support system. The first involves what would happen to people who exhausted their transitional benefits. There will be people who cannot find work, and there will be regions where few jobs are available. If government is not willing to provide cash support forever, it must provide full- or part-time jobs for those who exhaust transitional support, so that people can, in fact, support themselves. Just how many people would need these jobs is almost impossible to predict. Half of those who go on AFDC use it for more than two years. But that occurs in a world where there is no way to work part-time and escape poverty, where work does not pay well (both because wages are often low and because welfare benefits fall as earnings rise), and where there is little help or incentive to move off of welfare.

Only a tiny fraction might actually need these jobs if the other reforms were in place. Single mothers with child support would not have to work more than half-time to avoid poverty. And they would have had two to three years to adjust to their new situation, acquire training and transitional support, and move to a part-time private sector job. The program would certainly be considerably smaller than the current welfare system.

In reality, this proposal is not so different from that contained in the Family Support Act of 1988. Under that bill, people are required to participate in some activity—often jobs—starting almost immediately. These proposals may offer a workable alternative, especially in the short run. Yet it would be far better to make clear to all those concerned, both recipients and the public, that there are two separate programs: transitional assistance and jobs. Both programs will do their job better if they are separated.

Consider transitional support first. Currently most of those who use welfare use it for relatively short-term aid. Yet the first few years of welfare are not now considered "transitional." The same demands, rules, obligations, and indignities are put on the new recipient as the old one. The public does not perceive the difference between those who use welfare for temporary aid and those who use it for long-term assistance. Thus there is little dignity even in getting temporary help.

A system of transitional assistance could feel quite different. Transitional aid is unambiguously designed to help the recipient get on her or his feet. It is not a program to punish people for misbehaving, nor does it offer the hope that manipulating the system will lead to permanent support. Transitional support would be a second chance, an opportunity to take advantage of special aid. It is a chance to be taken advantage of, not another burden to get through just to gain enough aid to get by.

Those who study management say that organizations with a clear and unambiguous goal are most successful. A system that tries to train people and encourage self-support, demand work, and help the working poor, while simultaneously ensuring that people have some minimal income is one with very mixed goals. Ensuring income is quite different from encouraging self-support; the two are diametrically opposed. Not so for a transitional support system. The clear goal would be to help people help themselves.

After transitional support comes jobs. But isn't that the same as workfare? No. There is something fundamentally different about "working off a welfare check" and working at a community service job. In the first case you seem to be working for free, in the latter you are being paid for your work. Although participants in workfare programs express some satisfaction with the work, they think their employers are getting a very good deal. Similarly, when researchers recently asked welfare recipients about their attitudes toward workfare, they reported that "recipients like the idea that they would be working, but disliked the fact that they would still be on welfare." To both public and recipients, workfare will not be a job.

There will be much more pressure on both the transitional program and the jobs program to do their job well if they are separated. In a transitional program, it is easy to see how many people leave your program and when they do. It will also be easy to check to see how many people end up on the jobs program, because administrators would have to certify that clients had exhausted transitional assistance before they could get the jobs. In a workfare program, if there are not enough jobs, one just continues paying welfare. But in a jobs program, if there are not enough jobs, one knows immediately and there is an instant impetus to find more. A true jobs program will inevitably be more demanding than a workfare program. In workfare, one must go through an elaborate process of sanctions for people who fail to show up. With a job, when people don't work, they don't get paid.

Another problem with time-limited transitional aid is that some people are so dysfunctional, disabled, or their life is in such chaos that they cannot work. If half-time work at a minimum-wage job were sufficient to keep a single-parent family out of poverty, the number of such people would not be large. If people really cannot work, they ought to be on the SSI program for the disabled. Still, we will need some system for exempting and protecting people who truly cannot work. There will be people who need special, intensive services, who somehow don't qualify for the disability programs, but who cannot make it on their own. They need to be treated on a case-by-case basis. It would be a mistake, however, to design the entire support system worrying only about these people.

A final and far more difficult problem involves the period of adjustment as we move from one system to another. Giving insured child support benefits to anyone for whom a court order is not in place (or who has been exempted from it for good cause) is unwise, and therefore initially there will be a large number of people who do not have insured child support payments. If we moved rapidly to transitional assistance, the pressure on mothers, government agencies, and the courts to get awards in place would be enormous. In many ways that pressure would be useful—we would finally have created a strong incentive for finding all fathers. But in the interim, how do we protect mothers and children who do not yet have child support?

If transitional benefits lasted eighteen to thirty-six months, mothers and the state would have that long to work to get awards in place. Initially one might make the time limit on transitional benefits longer to give more time to identify fathers and get awards in place. Yet we may still find that fathers of children born many years earlier cannot readily be found.

Thus during the implementation phase, an insured benefit might be provided to anyone who is cooperating in good faith in the location and identification of the father. This provision would have to be written with considerable care, because it could be a very large loophole in the child support system. Finding fathers can be difficult and unpleasant. New York State has a variant on an insured benefit plan whereby benefits are only paid to people with awards in place, and there is enormous pressure to relax that requirement. The state and the clients need to have a very strong incentive to do child support enforcement. One might also force states to pick up a larger share of the cost of any insured benefit for someone who is making good faith efforts, but for whom no award is in place. Ultimately the "good faith" provision should be phased out, perhaps by insisting that new enrollees actually secure an award to qualify for an insured child support benefit.

People Who Play by the Rules Shouldn't Lose the Game

The message here is a simple one. If we want to reinforce our values of family, work, independence, and responsibility, we cannot allow working families to be the poorest of the poor. We cannot abide a system that traps women who want to work on welfare. We cannot let absent parents shirk their responsibilities.

We must ensure that if people work, they can achieve a measure of financial security. That means making work pay. And it means ensuring that single parents get some child support. For too long, the American dream has been an empty one for many of our children. We find generations of people mired in welfare with little hope and little sense that the future can be better. We see the costs of the despair in our schools and in our factories. To turn things around, we will have to ensure that people who play by the rules do not lose the game.

Appendix

Notes

References

Index

Appendix

This appendix presents information useful to interpret and reproduce the analysis of welfare dynamics in Chapter 2. The first section describes the data set used for the analysis and presents operational definitions of key concepts. The next section briefly reports some of the assumptions necessary to use hazard rate given limitations of the data. We include a somewhat more extensive discussion of our technique for studying repeat spells and total time on welfare. Finally, the appendix reports the regression results that underlie the spell analysis, and the analysis of exit reasons and impacts on spell duration and recidivism.

Data and Definitions

The data used for this study come from the twenty-one-year sample of the Panel Study of Income Dynamics (PSID), a longitudinal study that began with a sample of 5,000 families in 1968. The original sample was made up of two subsamples: a nationally representative sample of 3,000 families selected by the Survey Research Center at the University of Michigan, and a sample of 2,000 low-income families from the Survey of Economic Opportunity (SEO) conducted by the Census Bureau. The SEO oversampled low-income areas. The SEO subsample that became part of the PSID included households in which the head was under sixty-five and in which household income in 1967 was less than twice the Orshansky poverty ratio.

We use both subsamples in this study, in order to have a large enough number of AFDC recipients for analysis. The PSID assigned weights to the individuals in both samples, which are essentially the reciprocals of the probabilities of their being included in the original sample. (Weights are also adjusted to reflect sample nonresponse, but these adjustments are a relatively unimportant component of the weights.) We use these weights in all our analyses.

The PSID sample is described fully in Survey Research Center (1984). Its advantages and disadvantages are outlined in Urban Systems Research and Engineering (1982).

All of our analyses were performed on a subsample of the PSID that included all women who ever received welfare when they were female heads of households with children during the twenty-one study years that we looked at. Our major dependent variable was AFDC receipt. Though these terms might seem to be straightforward, there were several decisions we made in defining them that need to be noted.

Female Headship

We limited our analyses to women who received welfare when they were heads of households with children during the period of interest for analysis. By limiting our analyses to heads, we missed women who may have received AFDC for themselves and their children while they were living in someone else's household. By limiting our analyses to female heads, we effectively excluded AFDC-UP and AFDC received on behalf of step-children or foster children in male-headed families.

Having children was defined as the presence of children under age eighteen in the household. We do not know whether these children were the women's own, though we usually describe them as though they were.

AFDC Receipt

The first step in our analyses of AFDC receipt was to decide whether a female head had AFDC income during a given year. In general, if a female-headed household reported any AFDC income received by the head or wife (these were grouped together in PSID data collection; for our purposes only the head is relevant), we coded AFDC receipt during the year.

The decision to look only at the AFDC income of the head, rather than the total AFDC income of the household, seemed to us the best way to solve the subfamily problem, given the limitations of the data, which do not allow us to assign either children or AFDC income unambiguously to women who are not heads of households. The procedure does have its drawbacks, however. On the negative side, the receipt of AFDC income by a woman living with her child in her mother's household does not show up anywhere in our analysis: it is not attributed to the grandmother, assuming correct reporting, because it is not her own AFDC income; and it is not attributed to her daughter, because she is not a female head. We do not look at AFDC receipt until the daughter sets up her own household. Thus the AFDC spells of those daughters who never move out will be missed entirely, and the AFDC spells of those who do move out will look shorter than they really are. On the positive side, however, we do not falsely observe AFDC endings for the grandmothers when the daughters move out.

We made two adjustments to this basic procedure in defining AFDC receipt. Although there are separate questions for AFDC income, Supplemental Security Income, Social Security, and other welfare, it appears that a considerable amount of AFDC income is mistakenly reported as "other welfare." The strategy adopted here was to include other welfare income as AFDC income if the woman was a female head either at the beginning or end of the year in which the income was received, and if the woman reported receiving some AFDC income in at least one survey year.

To limit somewhat the possibility that persons who make very little use of welfare in the course of a year are treated as recipients, a minimum benefit threshold was used. In any year in which a woman received less welfare money than the maximum *monthly* benefit in her state (adjusted for family size), she was treated as receiving no welfare. In fact this threshold had very little effect, and eliminating it would have made very little difference. Nearly all persons who report welfare receipt in a year have rather sizable benefits.

Welfare Spells

The basic methodological construction used is that of continuous spells. A spell is a period of one or more years during which welfare is received "continuously." It is important to realize that persons classified as having a continuous spell of, say, four years may not have actually been on welfare nonstop for forty-eight months. There is information only on the total annual welfare income, not on how many months during the year a person received welfare income. Thus there is no way to classify periods of welfare receipt except by years in which income is received. In many ways to treat someone with a series of short spells as someone with a longer one is desirable, because persons who leave for only a very short period might be seen as being at least partially dependent on welfare throughout. Moreover, persons who leave for a few months owing to the "administrative churning" associated with the temporary failure to meet some administrative requirement are also treated as having continuous periods of receipt.

Beginning and Ending Events

Our assignment of beginning and especially ending events obviously involved decisions that have important effects on both our univariate and our multivariate analyses. Our general procedure was to look for "events" that occurred at the same time as a transition in or out of AFDC receipt or poverty. We looked for events in the following order, for transitions both in and out: relationship changes that affected eligibility; substantial changes in non-AFDC income; family size changes not related to AFDC eligibility; and geographical moves. If none of these events was found, we classified the beginning or ending as unexplained.

The first events we looked for were family composition changes of the sort that determine AFDC eligibility, that is, those related to female headship and to the presence of children. For beginnings we looked for transitions into the status of female head with child, from that of wife, child, other relative, or female head without child. For endings we looked for transitions out of the status of female head with child, to wife with child or female head without child. It should be noted again that we have not dealt in a very satisfactory way with subfamilies and multigenerational households. Ideally, we would have identified the change in status that takes place when a woman has her first child, whether or not she is at that time living in her own household. Instead, we coded the change in status that took place when a woman established her own household that included a child, whether the child was just born or several years old.

We looked for family composition changes related to AFDC eligibility both in the year of the transition and in the preceding year. We looked back a year primarily because family status was coded as of the time of the interview, sometime between March and June of a given year, while the income and AFDC data collected at the time referred to the previous calendar year. Imagine a woman who became a female head and went on welfare in February 1976. She therefore had AFDC income during calendar year 1976. We see her status in April 1977 as female head, but we also see her status in April 1976 as female head. If we did not look back to April 1975, we would wrongly miss the transition to female headship that indeed explained the transition to welfare receipt between calendar year 1975 and calendar year 1976.

Income Changes

The second event we looked for, if there had been no eligibility-related family composition change in the year of the transition or the year preceding, was substantial change in household income net of AFDC. We defined a "substantial" income change as an increase or decrease of $500 in 1978 dollars. We used this limit to exclude very small income fluctuations.

If we found a substantial change in non-AFDC income, we broke the change into three component parts: earnings of the head, earnings of others in the household, and non-AFDC transfer income. We identified the largest component, in dollars, and coded that as the transition type of interest.

Other Changes

The vast majority of transitions both into and out of both AFDC receipt and poverty were associated with either eligibility-related family composition changes or with substantial income changes. If we found neither, however, we next looked for two other sorts of changes. We first looked for family size changes not related to eligibility, usually the birth of new children. We hypothesized that the addition or the loss of household members could change the measured needs of the household enough to change income eligibility for AFDC. For beginnings we looked for an increase in family size, and for endings we looked for a decrease.

If we found no change in family size, we looked for a geographical move to a new county or state in the year of the transition or the year preceding. Again our thinking referred to AFDC eligibility: a family who moved would almost certainly go off AFDC for a time even if they later reestablished eligibility in the new jurisdiction. If we found no geographical move, after having found no other identifiable events, we classified the transition type as unidentified. The unidentified transitions may involve income changes below our threshold. They may also reflect decisions to participate or not to participate in the AFDC program that are independent of any of the events we looked for.

Hazard Rate Techniques

The analysis of Chapter 2 uses hazard rate techniques to describe the dynamics of welfare dependency. Hazard models now have considerable currency in social scientific research. The reader is referred to Paul Allison (1982, 1984) and John Kalbfleisch and Ross Prentice (1980) for useful introductions to the hazard models employed in our analysis. There is a more extensive introduction to our use of these methods in Urban Systems Research and Engineering (1982) and Bane and Ellwood (1983).

One limitation specific to our study is that our sample included only twenty-one years of usable data with which to calculate exit probabilities. We observed 1,000 first spells of AFDC recipiency.

Because of the number of exits and the right-censoring of cases for later entrants, the number of usable cases for persons with long spells of recipiency was too small to estimate exit probabilities for those in long spells with confidence.

As a result we were forced to make some assumptions about the exit probabilities in the later years. In spell years 14 through 16 the weighted exit probability appeared to remain level at about .10. We thus chose to assume that this rate was constant for durations up to 30 years. We assumed that no spell lasted more than 30 years. The resulting distributions are reported in Table 2.1.

These assumptions do not influence the distribution of completed spells for those beginning a spell of AFDC prior to those durations for which the assumption is made. It does have more impact on the other distributions, however. These distributions are somewhat sensitive to the assumption made. Under the current assumption of an exit probability of .10 for durations between 17 and 29 years, and 1.0 in the following year for all those who remain, 23.5 percent of all persons on AFDC at a point in time are in the midst of a spell that will last over 16 years, and the mean duration is 11.1 years. To take two extreme examples, if the assumed exit probability is .05, then some 25 percent of persons on the program are in the midst of spells exceeding 16 years, and the mean is 12 years. If the assumed value is .20, the figures are 21 percent and 10 years, respectively.

Return to Welfare and Total Time

Repeat spells and total time on welfare remain a seriously neglected and critically important subject of research on welfare dynamics. This section describes the assumptions that we used to classify spells as a first or repeat spell, to estimate rates of return to welfare, and to calculate total time durations that include first and repeat spells.

Classifying First and Later Spells of Welfare

In previous work, researchers have generally not distinguished carefully between first and later spells of welfare receipt. In part, this shortcoming is attributable to the lack of information in the data on whether the current spell of welfare is the first. For example, the PSID includes no information on presurvey welfare receipt. Therefore one cannot be certain whether the first observed spell of AFDC receipt is the true first spell.

The data in Table 2.2 suggest a straightforward way to estimate whether the first observed spell is in fact the first spell. The table reports the percentage who return to welfare after leaving it by elapsed time since the preceding spell. Return rates fall sharply after two years off the program. Thus, while 35 percent of first-time AFDC recipients will experience a subsequent spell of AFDC receipt, less than 15 percent of those who left AFDC more than three years earlier will return to AFDC, and about 7 percent of those whose previous spell ended six or more years ago will return. Consequently, if someone begins her first observed spell six or more years into the PSID, we can be relatively confident that this first observed spell is actually the true first spell. We can calculate the probability that the first observed spell is truly the first spell on the basis of the survey year in which the spell began. The likelihood that the first observed spell is the true first spell of AFDC receipt increases steadily as the continuous years of nonreceipt increase. The overwhelming proportion of first observed spells began after the first few years of the survey. Thus we can be fairly certain that most first observed spells are true first spells. For example, if we take a sample of all first observed spells in the PSID and omit those that began after only one observed year of not receiving welfare, then about 95 percent of our sample spells are likely to be true first spells.

Second and later spells are easy to classify if we group all later spells together. All observed second and later spells of AFDC receipt are obviously truly repeat spells. Although these spells can properly be classified as repeat spells, our ability to conduct separate analyses by the spell sequence was limited by the fact that few such spells were observed. It would be interesting to determine whether the durations of second spells were correlated with the durations of first spells of AFDC receipt. Making such a calculation is difficult, however, because it would require data on one complete spell and at least the beginnings of another. Serious sample selection problems are introduced because two complete spells are more likely to be observed if both spells are short.

Using Exit Probabilities to Estimate Total Welfare Time

The unweighted exit rates, unweighted standard errors, and sample sizes for all spells, for first spells, for later spells, and for recidivism are reported in Tables A.1, A.2, and A.3. Sample sizes and standard errors are generally quite reasonable, except for later years of later spells, as already discussed.

These exit probabilities were used to derive completed spell distributions. For notation, let $P1(t)$ = the proportion of persons who have a first spell of exactly t years. Let $P2(t)$ be the probability that someone having a later spell has one that lasts exactly t years. And let $PR(t)$ be the probability that a person who has ended a spell returns in year t. The corresponding cumulative distributions are $C1(t)$, $C2(t)$, and $CR(t)$.

Table A.1 Sample sizes, unweighted probabilities, and standard errors for first spells

Outcome measure	Unweighted probability	Standard error	Sample size
Year 1	0.25	0.014	1,000
Year 2	0.21	0.015	701
Year 3	0.17	0.016	518
Year 4	0.19	0.019	411
Year 5	0.15	0.020	312
Year 6	0.15	0.023	244
Year 7	0.12	0.023	189
Year 8	0.14	0.028	146
Year 9	0.10	0.028	120
Year 10	0.14	0.018	358

Table A.2 Sample sizes, unweighted probabilities, and standard errors for repeat spells

Outcome measure	Unweighted probability	Standard error	Sample size
Year 1	0.31	0.020	549
Year 2	0.27	0.024	339
Year 3	0.20	0.027	221
Year 4	0.22	0.032	165
Year 5	0.18	0.035	120
Year 6	0.21	0.043	92
Year 7	0.19	0.049	63
Year 8	0.21	0.059	47
Year 9	0.13	0.057	34
Year 10	0.18	0.038	102

Table A.3 Sample sizes, unweighted probabilities, and standard errors for recidivism

Outcome measure	Unweighted probability	Standard error	Sample size
Year 1	0.20	0.011	1,438
Year 2	0.08	0.008	1,092
Year 3	0.05	0.007	950
Year 4	0.04	0.007	840
Year 5	0.03	0.006	745
Year 6	0.03	0.007	662
Year 7	0.01	0.005	586
Year 8	0.02	0.006	529
Year 9	0.01	0.005	472
Year 10	0.00	0.001	2,084

The goal is to determine how many persons have total welfare time of exactly s years within a window of 25 years. Any spell that is not over by 25 years after the beginning of the first spell is assumed to end at that time. The window is an arbitrary choice. The calculation of the number of persons who have total welfare time of s years is simply a matter of figuring out all the combinations of first and later spells that would lead to exactly s years of total welfare.

The key assumption is that the distributions of first and later spells and recidivism are independent. If so, it is a straightforward matter to calculate the probability of any particular combination that yields exactly s years of welfare. We assumed that a person would have no more than three spells of welfare receipt. Although there are more compact ways to represent the formulas, the easiest way to understand the method is to break down the probability that someone spends exactly s years in total time into the sum of: the probability that she will have exactly three completed spells lasting s years [$PC3(s)$]; plus the probability that she will have exactly two completed spells lasting s years [$PC2(s)$]; plus the probability that she will have exactly one spell lasting s years [$PC1(s)$]; plus the probability that she will have two complete spells and one spell that is uncompleted in year 24 after beginning [$PU3(s)$]; plus the odds that she has one complete and one incomplete spell [$PU2(s)$]. A woman can have a single incomplete spell only if $s = 25$. The formula for each possibility is given below.

Three complete spells

$$PC3(s) = \sum_{j=1}^{s-2} [P1(j) \sum_{i=1}^{s-j-1} P2(i) \, P2(s-j-i)] \sum_{k=1}^{25-s-2} PR(k) CR(25-s-k-1).$$

Two complete spells

$$PC2(s) = \sum_{j=1}^{k-1} P1(j) \, [P2(s-j)] \sum_{k=1}^{25-s-1} PR(k) \, [1 - CR(25-s-k-1)].$$

One complete spell

$$PC1(s) = P1(s)\,[1 - CR(25 - s - 1)].$$

Two complete and one incomplete spell

$$PU3(s) = \sum_{j=1}^{s-2} \{P1(j) \sum_{i=1}^{s-j-1} P2(1)\,[1 - C2(s-j-i-1)]\}$$

$$\sum_{k=1}^{25-s-1} PR(25 - s - k - 1).$$

One complete and one incomplete spell

$$PU2(s) = \sum_{j=1}^{s-1} P1(j)\quad [1 - C2(s-j-1)]PR(25-s).$$

One incomplete spell

$$PU1(s) = 1 - C1(24) \qquad \text{if } s = 25,$$

otherwise

$$PU1(s) = 0.$$

Thus, $PTOT(s)$, the probability that a person has total welfare time lasting exactly s years, is:

$$PTOT(s) = PC3(s) + PC2(s) + PC1(s) + PU3(s) + PU2(s) + PU1(s).$$

The PTOT distribution can then be treated exactly as if it were a distribution of completed spells. All other distributions are derived in the same way, assuming one has a distribution of completed spells. Tables 2.3 and 2.10 report some distributions from these calculations.

The Logit Estimates and the Simulation Model

We used logit models to estimate exit rates and recidivism rates. The coefficients used to prepare the estimates of marginal impacts (Table 2.4) are provided in Tables A.4, A.5, and A.6. The means used to prepare that table are reported in Table A.7. All logit equations were run unweighted.

Table A.4 Logistic regression coefficients for first-spell duration (used for Tables 2.4, 2.5, 2.6)

Variable	Coefficient	Standard error
black	−0.382	0.129
other	−0.112	0.304
no high school	−0.491	0.183
high school dropout	−0.452	0.104
married	1.092	0.356
single	−0.715	0.171
widowed	0.780	0.301
separated	−0.432	0.161
northeast	0.060	0.174
north central	−0.435	0.158
south	0.096	0.181
fmax[a]	−0.014	0.035
age 22 to 30	−0.059	0.120
age 31 to 40	−0.099	0.204
age over 40	0.182	0.237
2 to 3 children	−0.043	0.111
4 or more children	−0.140	0.238
work experience	0.368	0.106
youngest 3 to 5 yrs	0.018	0.126
youngest 6 to 10 yrs	0.164	0.156

Table A.4 (continued)

Variable	Coefficient	Standard error
youngest 11 yrs +	0.397	0.243
disabled	−0.491	0.136
length 2 years	0.089	0.131
length 3 years	−0.271	0.158
length 4 years	−0.077	0.170
length 5 years	−0.355	0.208
length 6 years	−0.195	0.222
length 7 years	−0.399	0.265
length 8 years	−0.412	0.298
length 9 plus years	−0.390	0.212
year 73	0.513	0.269
year 74	0.114	0.290
year 75	0.426	0.268
year 76	0.318	0.266
year 77	0.511	0.254
year 78	0.005	0.280
year 79	0.635	0.251
year 80	0.540	0.254
year 81	0.186	0.275
year 82	0.353	0.270
year 83	0.202	0.273
year 84	0.511	0.263
year 85	0.602	0.265
year 86	0.383	0.275
year 87	0.434	0.282
constant	−0.555	0.373

a. Maximum AFDC benefits in hundreds of dollars.

For the simulation model, a slightly more restricted set of variables was used in the recidivism and later-spell logit equations. The coefficients used for simulation are provided in Tables A.8 and A.9. The simulation model used a sample of all persons who began a first

Table A.5 Logistic regression coefficients used to estimate marginal impact of variables on recidivism (Table 2.4)

Variable	Coefficient	Standard error
black	0.553	0.163
other	0.338	0.429
no high school	0.377	0.189
high school dropout	0.384	0.131
married	0.070	0.343
single	0.324	0.172
widowed	0.086	0.224
separated	0.117	0.167
northeast	0.711	0.230
north central	0.328	0.221
south	0.354	0.255
fmax	0.017	0.043
age 22 to 30	−0.060	0.233
age 31 to 40	−0.486	0.272
age over 40	−0.506	0.273
2 to 3 children	0.589	0.135
4 or more children	0.350	0.285
work experience	−0.219	0.128
youngest 3 to 5 yrs	0.403	0.162
youngest 6 to 10 yrs	0.558	0.157
youngest 11 yrs +	0.290	0.180
disabled	0.064	0.157
length 2 years	−0.937	0.158
length 3 years	−1.339	0.197
length 4 years	−1.682	0.247
length 5 years	−1.515	0.249
length 6 years	−1.882	0.312
length 7 years	−2.800	0.516
length 8 years	−2.183	0.430
length 9 plus years	−3.481	0.431
year 70	−1.053	0.689

Table A.5   (continued)

Variable	Coefficient	Standard error
year 71	−0.394	0.609
year 72	−1.802	0.702
year 73	−0.837	0.559
year 74	−1.094	0.551
year 75	−1.252	0.546
year 76	−1.762	0.566
year 77	−1.193	0.525
year 78	−1.298	0.524
year 79	−1.351	0.530
year 80	−0.676	0.508
year 81	−1.029	0.514
year 82	−0.973	0.515
year 83	−1.120	0.519
year 84	−1.552	0.536
year 85	−1.173	0.517
year 86	−1.148	0.518
year 87	−1.139	0.522
constant	−1.538	0.646

spell. Each person's characteristics were plugged into the logit equations represented in Tables A.4, A.8, and A.9 to predict exit probabilities for first and later spells and for recidivism. The age of the mother was assumed to increase by 5 years from the beginning age in the recidivism equation, and by 10 years in the later-spell equation. Number of children, work experience, and age of youngest children were dropped for later spells and recidivism, because it is extremely difficult to estimate changes in the number of children or their ages without using elaborate models that are beyond the scope of this analysis. Once these exit probabilities were generated, a PTOT distribution similar to the one already given was generated for each person. These were then tabulated according to whatever groupings were selected.

Table A.6 Logistic regression coefficients used to estimate marginal impact of variables on repeat spell duration (Table 2.4)

Variable	Coefficient	Standard error
black	0.053	0.584
other	0.223	0.618
no high school	−0.130	0.248
high school dropout	−0.170	0.168
married	1.650	0.660
single	0.190	0.210
widowed	0.306	0.278
separated	−0.249	0.205
northeast	−0.321	0.304
north central	−0.324	0.292
south	−0.103	0.347
fmax	−0.057	0.054
age 22 to 30	0.308	0.409
age 31 to 40	0.805	0.451
age over 40	1.067	0.461
2 to 3 children	−0.027	0.177
4 or more children	−0.142	0.331
work experience	−0.023	0.162
youngest 3 to 5 yrs	−0.097	0.221
youngest 6 to 10 yrs	−0.213	0.204
youngest 11 yrs +	−0.401	0.249
disabled	−0.034	0.185
length 2 years	−0.067	0.191
length 3 years	−0.462	0.236
length 4 years	−0.430	0.273
length 5 years	−0.363	0.311
length 6 years	−0.614	0.412
length 7 years	−0.299	0.454
length 8 years	−0.659	0.609
length 9 plus years	−0.385	0.401
year 72	1.020	0.967
year 73	0.846	0.983

Table A.6   (continued)

Variable	Coefficient	Standard error
year 74	0.804	0.935
year 75	0.875	0.914
year 76	1.370	0.894
year 77	1.840	0.898
year 78	1.539	0.895
year 79	1.056	0.895
year 80	1.115	0.888
year 81	1.227	0.874
year 82	1.282	0.871
year 83	1.401	0.871
year 84	1.369	0.876
year 85	1.333	0.880
year 86	1.593	0.874
year 87	1.180	0.879
constant	−1.851	1.126

Exit Reasons: Multinomial Logit

In order to characterize the dynamics of dependence for different types of people and to isolate the independent impact of a variety of explanatory variables, we sought a method that would allow us to estimate duration-dependent exit probabilities that separated the path or type of exit. The assumption we felt most comfortable with was one that might be labeled a "proportional probabilities" approach. We were willing to assume that each explanatory variable raised or lowered the likelihood of exiting by one path by a fixed proportion regardless of the duration of the spell to date. A multinomial logit model comes very close to providing the desired estimates. (See McFadden [1973, 1976] and Nerlove and Press [1973] for more complete information.)

In principle a multinomial logit model could be estimated separately for each year a spell had progressed and the assumption of "proportional probabilities" could be relaxed. Thus we could use the

*Table A.*7 Sample means used to estimate marginal impact of variables on
duration, recidivism (Table 2.4)

Variable	Sample means		
	First spells	Recidivism	Repeat spells
black	0.760	0.773	0.826
other	0.035	0.033	0.158
no high school	0.126	0.166	0.193
high school dropout	0.415	0.314	0.399
married	0.039	0.037	0.023
single	0.449	0.290	0.271
widowed	0.078	0.104	0.142
separated	0.295	0.254	0.289
northeast	0.131	0.141	0.154
north central	0.254	0.236	0.229
south	0.472	0.469	0.495
fmax[a]	4.495	4.480	4.449
age 22 to 30	0.406	0.347	0.408
age 31 to 40	0.141	0.194	0.236
age over 40	0.147	0.404	0.326
2 to 3 children	0.414	0.372	0.530
4 or more children	0.145	0.254	0.161
work experience	0.675	0.631	0.649
youngest 3 to 5 yrs	0.220	0.190	0.179
youngest 6 to 10 yrs	0.159	0.197	0.291
youngest 11 yrs +	0.066	0.285	0.222
disabled	0.194	0.228	0.292
year 70	—	0.022	—
year 71	—	0.022	—
year 72	—	0.036	0.030
year 73	0.072	0.041	0.028
year 74	0.053	0.050	0.048
year 75	0.055	0.049	0.048
year 76	0.062	0.054	0.044
year 77	0.071	0.066	0.030
year 78	0.044	0.061	0.057
year 79	0.063	0.054	0.067
year 80	0.061	0.067	0.055
year 81	0.045	0.064	0.101
year 82	0.048	0.059	0.078

Table A.7 *(continued)*

Variable	Sample means		
	First spells	Recidivism	Repeat spells
year 83	0.054	0.064	0.083
year 84	0.051	0.060	0.073
year 85	0.053	0.067	0.053
year 86	0.039	0.066	0.076
year 87	0.031	0.060	0.076

a. Adjusted maximum AFDC benefit in hundreds of dollars.

model to estimate the impact of various independent variables on the probability of exit via a particular route in the first year of a spell. Then a second equation could be estimated for those in the second year of a spell and so forth. Unfortunately we had far too little data to create such estimates, and thus turned to the "proportional probabilities" assumption.

We were forced to combine years. To estimate our model each person-year of a spell was a separate observation. Some individuals entered several times, once in the first year of their spell, again in their second year and so forth. Dummy variables were included indicating the length of spell to date. Thus for each type of exit we allow a different base (or intercept) exit probability for each year of the spell. Independent variables alter that base probability. There were insufficient observations to estimate the exit probabilities beyond year 10. Thus for years 9 to 25 we assumed that the exit probability equaled the average of years 9 and 10.

This approach has several undesirable features. The most obvious one is that some individuals enter the models several times. There is no avoiding their repeated inclusion. We can only observe a recipient in the second year of a spell if the person was previously in the first year. Indeed all of the duration-dependent exit probabilities included persons with long spells in the estimates of several exit probabilities. Including these individuals repeatedly causes no problems if there are no individual differences in exit probabilities that persist over time that are not captured by the measured vari-

Table A.8 Logistic regression coefficients for recidivism (used for simulation model, Tables 2.5, 2.6)

Variable	Coefficient	Standard error
black	0.567	0.162
other	0.245	0.424
no high school	0.331	0.187
high school dropout	0.375	0.128
married	0.004	0.342
single	0.213	0.169
widowed	0.072	0.221
separated	0.039	0.165
northeast	0.758	0.227
north central	0.412	0.217
south	0.613	0.241
fmax	0.088	0.039
age 22 to 30	0.076	0.228
age 31 to 40	−0.378	0.260
age over 40	−0.618	0.264
disabled	0.014	0.152
length 2 years	−0.969	0.157
length 3 years	−1.391	0.195
length 4 years	−1.742	0.246
length 5 years	−1.592	0.248
length 6 years	−1.956	0.311
length 7 years	−2.889	0.514
length 8 years	−2.273	0.428
length 9 plus years	−3.616	0.430
year 70	−1.135	0.682
year 71	−0.502	0.604
year 72	−1.833	0.698
year 73	−0.975	0.554
year 74	−1.140	0.544
year 75	−1.223	0.539
year 76	−1.767	0.559
year 77	−1.261	0.519

Table A.8 *(continued)*

Variable	Coefficient	Standard error
year 78	−1.334	0.517
year 79	−1.410	0.523
year 80	−0.670	0.501
year 81	−1.012	0.507
year 82	−0.975	0.508
year 83	−1.074	0.513
year 84	−1.508	0.529
year 85	−1.161	0.510
year 86	−1.117	0.510
year 87	−1.098	0.515
constant	−1.526	0.618

ables. If there are no unmeasured persistent differences, then the estimated coefficients and standard errors are correct. It seems likely, however, that some heterogeneity remains that is not captured by the independent variables.

The most serious problem that heterogeneity causes is that the standard errors of the estimated coefficients are probably too small—variables look more significant than they are. The standard errors are based on the assumption that each observation is independent. But some persons enter several times in different years in their spells. If these people have persistent unmeasured differences, a kind of serial correlation is created, and standard errors are understated. We report the standard errors as they are calculated normally. The reader should remember that they are likely downward biased.

As is well known, heterogeneity causes other problems as well. Its presence obscures the interpretation of declining exit probabilities. It also raises questions about whether we should expect coefficients on the measured variables to be constant as time on the spell increases. There now exists a growing literature in economics that uses continuous hazard functions to examine dynamics. Unfortunately, in these models, heterogeneity must either be ignored or it

Table A.9   Logistic regression coefficients for repeat spell duration (used for simulation model, Tables 2.5, 2.6)

Variable	Coefficient	Standard error
black	0.117	0.573
other	0.030	0.603
no high school	−0.133	0.241
high school dropout	−0.164	0.166
married	1.577	0.652
single	0.194	0.208
widowed	0.278	0.274
separated	−0.231	0.203
northeast	−0.268	0.299
north central	−0.256	0.283
south	−0.037	0.330
fmax	−0.049	0.049
age 22 to 30	0.215	0.393
age 31 to 40	0.575	0.419
age over 40	0.826	0.427
disabled	−0.015	0.183
length 2 years	−0.079	0.191
length 3 years	−0.481	0.235
length 4 years	−0.441	0.272
length 5 years	−0.363	0.310
length 6 years	−0.608	0.409
length 7 years	−0.292	0.452
length 8 years	−0.691	0.611
length 9 plus years	−0.449	0.396
year 72	1.106	0.962
year 73	0.909	0.979
year 74	0.919	0.928
year 75	0.966	0.909
year 76	1.456	0.889
year 77	1.935	0.892
year 78	1.634	0.889
year 79	1.139	0.890
year 80	1.220	0.882

Table A.9 *(continued)*

Variable	Coefficient	Standard error
year 81	1.358	0.866
year 82	1.405	0.864
year 83	1.520	0.864
year 84	1.486	0.869
year 85	1.431	0.874
year 86	1.688	0.868
year 87	1.281	0.872
constant	−1.933	1.110

must be modeled explicitly. There is evidence that estimates are sensitive to the way in which heterogeneity is modeled (Blank 1986; Heckman and Singer 1982, 1984; Lancaster 1979).

We believe it would be valuable to test the sensitivity of our basic results to other types of specifications. We doubt that the qualitative results would be affected, but it would be interesting to know how robust the quantitative results are to functional form. We want to emphasize that our models are best thought of as descriptions. They are not intended to be used to predict the impact of massive changes. We do not pretend to have captured causal impacts. The models that we estimate should be treated with caution and seen as an inexact preliminary representation of the dynamics of dependence.

Our regression results and the measured standard errors for the multinomial logit model for type of exits are presented in Tables A.10, A.11, and A.12. The reader is again reminded that our measured standard errors are probably low. The results are based on unweighted multinomial logit methods. We actually tried several weighting methods and the results were largely unaffected. Because the performance of weighted multinomial logit in this type of circumstance is somewhat uncertain, and because the results seem unaffected by the weights, we chose to use the unweighted results. This is another area for further exploration.

Table A.10 Multinomial logit coefficients by exit reason: Marriage exits

Variable	Coefficient	Standard error
black	−1.669	0.284
other	0.585	0.488
no high school	−0.819	0.424
high school dropout	−0.646	0.254
married	2.684	0.563
single	−0.916	0.372
widowed	N.A.*	N.A.
separated	−0.307	0.339
northeast	−0.089	0.405
north central	−0.697	0.393
south	−0.207	0.452
fmax	−0.250	0.094
age 22 to 30	−0.194	0.276
age 31 to 40	−0.144	0.474
age over 40	−0.976	0.753
2 to 3 children	−0.315	0.263
4 or more children	0.351	0.549
work experience	0.294	0.262
youngest 3 to 5 yrs	0.119	0.287
youngest 6 to 10 yrs	−0.083	0.415
youngest 11 yrs +	0.471	0.756
disabled	−0.346	0.314
length 2 years	0.586	0.340
length 3 years	1.167	0.346
length 4 years	1.248	0.389
length 5 years	0.516	0.542
length 6 years	1.318	0.500
length 7 years	0.636	0.668
length 8 years	0.408	0.789
length 9 plus years	−0.561	0.798
year 73	−0.408	0.669
year 74	−0.624	0.674
year 75	−0.583	0.631

Table A.10　(continued)

Variable	Coefficient	Standard error
year 76	−1.123	0.673
year 77	−0.277	0.547
year 78	−1.182	0.650
year 79	*N.A.*	*N.A.*
year 80	−1.402	0.660
year 81	−0.947	0.637
year 82	−0.590	0.596
year 83	−0.809	0.609
year 84	−0.714	0.612
year 85	−0.137	0.575
year 86	−0.803	0.632
year 87	−0.566	0.619
constant	0.339	0.855

* *N.A.* = Not available; cell size too small to produce reliable estimates.

Table A.11 Multinomial logit coefficients by exit reason: Earnings exits

Variable	Coefficient	Standard error
black	−0.412	0.313
other	−1.226	1.077
no high school	−1.142	0.645
high school dropout	−0.581	0.253
married	N.A.*	N.A.
single	−0.807	0.353
widowed	−0.806	1.119
separated	−1.003	0.357
northeast	−0.423	0.439
north central	−0.670	0.382
south	−0.405	0.465
fmax	−0.100	0.092
age 22 to 30	0.279	0.295
age 31 to 40	0.306	0.490
age over 40	0.741	0.556
2 to 3 children	−0.302	0.273
4 or more children	0.508	0.502
work experience	0.888	0.311
youngest 3 to 5 yrs	0.256	0.289
youngest 6 to 10 yrs	0.169	0.364
youngest 11 yrs +	−0.005	0.722
disabled	−0.829	0.387
length 2 years	−0.417	0.300
length 3 years	−1.061	0.427
length 4 years	−0.679	0.431
length 5 years	−0.716	0.502
length 6 years	−1.459	0.747
length 7 years	−1.816	1.031
length 8 years	−0.526	0.639
length 9 plus years	−1.995	0.771
year 73	0.729	0.847
year 74	0.660	0.848
year 75	0.563	0.849

Table A.11   *(continued)*

Variable	Coefficient	Standard error
year 76	1.280	0.726
year 77	0.790	0.765
year 78	1.146	0.747
year 79	0.883	0.772
year 80	1.047	0.736
year 81	1.198	0.742
year 82	0.623	0.817
year 83	0.524	0.815
year 84	−0.151	0.958
year 85	1.893	0.706
year 86	0.784	0.795
year 87	1.569	0.744
constant	−2.191	1.018

* *N.A.* = Not available; cell size too small to produce reliable estimate.

Table A.12 Multinomial logit coefficients by exit reason: Other

Variable	Coefficient	Standard error
black	−0.097	0.152
other	−0.333	0.389
no high school	−0.340	0.205
high school dropout	−0.377	0.119
married	0.942	0.403
single	−0.629	0.203
widowed	1.022	0.323
separated	−0.319	0.190
northeast	0.122	0.197
north central	−0.376	0.180
south	0.199	0.203
fmax	0.036	0.040
age 22 to 30	−0.091	0.139
age 31 to 40	−0.148	0.234
age over 40	0.234	0.264
2 to 3 children	0.029	0.127
4 or more children	−0.359	0.283
work experience	0.304	0.120
youngest 3 to 5 yrs	−0.055	0.146
youngest 6 to 10 yrs	0.227	0.175
youngest 11 yrs +	0.476	0.260
disabled	−0.487	0.155
length 2 years	0.125	0.149
length 3 years	−0.435	0.188
length 4 years	−0.190	0.198
length 5 years	−0.386	0.238
length 6 years	−0.242	0.254
length 7 years	−0.339	0.292
length 8 years	−0.484	0.350
length 9 plus years	−0.160	0.229
year 73	0.647	0.295
year 74	0.163	0.329
year 75	0.577	0.298

Table A.12   (continued)

Variable	Coefficient	Standard error
year 76	0.394	0.303
year 77	0.593	0.289
year 78	−0.016	0.329
year 79	0.991	0.274
year 80	0.775	0.282
year 81	0.162	0.322
year 82	0.444	0.307
year 83	0.318	0.309
year 84	0.753	0.293
year 85	0.349	0.321
year 86	0.510	0.312
year 87	0.320	0.336
constant	−1.603	0.429

Notes

1. The Context for Welfare Reform

1. Error rates obtained from unpublished tables provided by the Family Support Administration, Office of Family Assistance, Division of Quality Control.

2. Before the Omnibus Budget Reconciliation Act (OBRA), the first $30 of earnings, plus one third of the remainder, plus all work expenses, were disregarded for the purpose of calculating AFDC benefits. OBRA limited work expenses to $75 per month, and allowed the "thirty and a third" to be disregarded for only four months. Families with a gross income greater than 150 percent of the state's standard of need were denied eligibility for benefits, whatever their net income. Revisions in 1984 loosened these restrictions somewhat, raising the gross income level to 185 percent of the standard of need, and extending the $30 part of "thirty and a third" for eight months beyond the earlier four-month limit.

3. O'Neill (1990) and Nightingale et al. (1991) have recently evaluated the program. Nightingale and her colleagues find modest positive effects on welfare receipt, employment, and earnings; O'Neill finds little or no effect of the program.

4. The FSA does make one important change in eligibility that is worth noting here: it requires all states to establish AFDC-UP programs for unemployed parents. There is less to this requirement than meets the eye, however, because all the large states already had AFDC-UP programs, and AFDC-UP clients are a relatively small part of the caseload everywhere.

5. Bane (1989) has argued that voluntary and mandatory programs both carry their own dangers, and that both types of programs can be implemented successfully. The dangers of welfare workers falling into paper compliance routines under a mandatory program, however, seem real.

6. Basically, the federal government will pay 90 percent of the costs of

195

JOBS programs up to the amount of states' WIN appropriations, plus additional funding estimated at about one billion dollars for JOBS personnel. Child care is an open-ended entitlement at the Medicaid matching rate (U.S House 1992, pp. 614–615).

2. Understanding Welfare Dynamics

1. The PSID study is described in a user's guide (Survey Research Center 1984). Its appropriateness for this study was discussed in Urban Systems Research and Engineering (1982).

2. Measuring characteristics at the beginning is helpful for making predictions such as those used in Table 2.5 and in estimating total time. Many characteristics change over the course of a spell, however. For example, both mother and children age, new children may enter the household, and disability status can change. When we estimate a model that allows these to vary over the course of the spell, several variables, particularly disability status and number of children, become more powerful.

3. Work by O'Neill et al. (1984), using a different data set, suggests a more important role for the age of the youngest child. We have not been able to explain the divergent estimates. These differences, together with the fact that our estimates are very sensitive to specification, suggest that this is an area that merits further investigation.

4. The Appendix discusses the methods used for developing these aggregate estimates of total welfare time.

5. This distribution of beginning types is estimated from 554 observed beginnings.

6. Our procedure raises the question of whether family changes and earnings changes might have occurred at the same time, and whether our procedure underestimates the importance of earnings by giving family changes priority. This is certainly possible, but it seems to us quite likely that any earnings changes we observe in these cases will be related to the associated family structure changes. This might be an interesting issue for further research, however.

7. The majority of women who become female heads while not living with their husbands have in fact never been married. The term "acquired" is used because not all of these women are the birth mothers of the children that now allow them to receive AFDC.

8. In most cases the results are very similar to those found by Ellwood

and Bane (1985). However, a coding error in the original version of the Bane and Ellwood paper had the effect of causing some people who left when transfers to them from other sources grew (such as Social Security Survivors Benefits or child support payments) to show up as leaving due to earnings. These results correct that error.

9. Other classification schemes also suggest the earnings may be more important than the 25 percent suggested using the Bane-Ellwood classification. For example, over 40 percent of all persons who left welfare, and for whom a beginning could be observed, had an earnings gain of more than $2,000 between the year they began and the year they left.

10. Women who had children under age six when they began receiving welfare account for 83 percent of the recipients at any point in time.

11. Current research by the Rockefeller Foundation's Minority Female Single Parents employment and training demonstration program and related work sponsored by the Women's Bureau of the U.S. Department of Labor are addressing the issue of child-care barriers to employment training and economic self-sufficiency.

12. The Family Support Act extends employment and training services to women with children aged three or over. The act also targets services toward (1) recipients who received AFDC for thirty-six of the past sixty months; (2) parents under age twenty-four who have not completed high school or who have little work experience in the previous year; and (3) members of families within two years of losing eligibility because of the age of their youngest child.

3. Understanding Dependency

1. If she spends down her "excess income" on medical care costs she would become eligible for Medicaid in this state.

2. This discussion draws heavily on the excellent review article by Rainwater (1987).

3. The differences are even larger when one looks at an entire year. In 1991, some 40 percent of single parents worked full-year full-time while 35 percent of married mothers did. By contrast, 30 percent of female heads worked part of the year as opposed to 38 percent for married mothers (U.S. Bureau of the Census 1992, table 14).

4. There are two sources of "contrary" evidence. Heidi Spalter-Roth et al. (1991) found, using data from the Survey of Income and Program Participation (SIPP), that 17 percent of women who used welfare over

a two-year period combined work and welfare in at least one month. Christopher Jencks and Kathryn Edin (1990) report that nearly all women in a nonrandom set of case studies supplemented their income with "off-the-book" earnings. Note that for these purposes, however, the program data are what is relevant, because the distinctions between models were made under the implicit assumption that earnings were to be reported.

5. The studies are actually quite different. Lerman's focused on ghetto youth who were still at home. Hill and Ponza examined all youth after most had left home.

6. Even these figures misstate the fall. During this period average family size was also falling, from 4 persons per case to 3. Because benefits are adjusted for family size, the actual cut in money received was considerably greater.

7. Inferred from table 15, U.S. Bureau of the Census (1985a). The number of poor children in female-headed families increased by 1.7 million.

4. Increasing Self-Sufficiency by Reforming Welfare

1. These two authors are particularly interesting to look at because they come to similar conclusions about the importance of management from quite different political perspectives, Mead being a conservative advocate of work obligations and Behn a more liberal proponent of the ET approach.

2. This phrase, as well as many of the ideas in this section, reflects the work of Toby Herr and Project Match. They are elegantly documented and explained in Herr, Halpern, and Conrad (1991).

3. This section relies heavily on Bane and Dowling (1985). That paper drew on the experience of the authors with the New York State welfare system, where both worked as welfare administrators at the time.

4. These calculations are based on AFDC and food stamp levels reported in U.S. House, Ways and Means (1992). Food stamps for housing assistance recipients were calculated by omitting the excess shelter exemption, which was assumed at the maximum in food stamps calculations for other recipients. No account was taken of the fact that some states reduce AFDC benefit levels for public housing residents, so the estimates for them may be a bit high. It was assumed that food stamps were spent for food and that the first call on the AFDC check was to bring food spending up to the food stamp level of $292. It was then

assumed that AFDC income was spent for rent, and that anything left over was for "other." Total spending was assumed to equal the sum of food stamps and AFDC; when the costs of food and rent exceeded total income, negative discretionary income was calculated to balance the books.

References

Aber, J. Lawrence, LaRue Allen, Robin Garfinkel, Christina Mitchell, and Edward Seidman. 1992. "Indices of Neighborhood Impoverishment: Their Association with Mental Health and School Achievement." Paper presented at the Conference on the Urban Underclass, University of Michigan, June.

ACIR. *See* Advisory Commission on Intergovernmental Relations.

Advisory Commission on Intergovernmental Relations. 1980. *The Federal Role in the Federal System: The Dynamics of Growth; Public Assistance: The Growth of a Federal Function.* Washington, D.C.: Government Printing Office.

Allison, Paul D. 1982. "Discrete-Time Methods for the Analysis of Event Histories." In S. Leinhardt, ed., *Sociological Methodology 1982.* San Francisco: Jossey-Bass.

———— 1984. Event History Analysis. *Regression for Longitudinal Event Data.* Sage University Paper Series on Quantitative Applications in the Social Sciences, no. 07–046. Beverly Hills: Sage Publications.

Andrisani, Paul J. 1978. *Work Attitudes and Labor Market Experience.* New York: Praeger.

———— 1981. "Reply" (to Duncan and Morgan). *Journal of Human Resources,* 16: 659–666.

Atkinson, J. W. 1964. *An Introduction to Motivation.* Princeton, N.J.: D. Van Nostrand.

Auletta, Ken. 1982. *The Underclass.* New York: Random House.

Bane, Mary Jo. 1989. "Welfare Reform and Mandatory versus Voluntary Work: Policy Issue or Management Problem?" *Journal of Policy Analysis and Management,* 8: 285–289.

Bane, Mary Jo, and Michael Dowling. 1985. "Trends in the Administration of Welfare Programs." Paper presented to the Association for Public Policy Analysis and Management, Washington, D.C.

Bane, Mary Jo, and David T. Ellwood. 1983. "The Dynamics of Dependence: The Routes to Self-Sufficiency." Report to the U.S. Department of Health and Human Services. Cambridge, Mass.: Urban Systems Research and Engineering.

Bassi, Laurie J. 1987. "Family Structure and Poverty among Women and Children: What Accounts for the Change?" Georgetown University, Washington, D.C., June. Mimeo.

Becker, Gary S. 1973. "Theory of Marriage, Part I." *Journal of Political Economy*, 81: 813–846.

———— 1981. *A Treatise on the Family*. Cambridge, Mass.: Harvard University Press.

Behn, Robert D. 1987. "Managing Innovation in Welfare, Training, and Work: Some Lessons from ET Choices in Massachusetts." Paper presented at the annual meetings of the American Political Science Association.

———— 1991. *Leadership Counts: Lessons for Public Managers from the Massachusetts Welfare, Training, and Employment Program*. Cambridge, Mass.: Harvard University Press.

Bell, Winifred. 1973. "Too Few Services to Separate." *Social Work*, 18: 66–77.

Blank, Rebecca. 1986. "How Important Is Welfare Dependence?" Princeton University. Mimeo.

———— 1989. "The Effect of Medical Need and Medicaid on AFDC Participation." *Journal of Human Resources*, 24: 54–87.

Bloom, Dan, Veronica Fellerath, David Long, and Robert G. Wood. 1993. *LEAP: Interim Findings on a Welfare Initiative to Improve School Attendance among Teenage Parents: Ohio's Learning, Earning, and Parenting Program*. New York: Manpower Demonstration Research Corporation.

Brodkin, Evelyn Z. 1986. *The False Promise of Administrative Reform: Implementing Quality Control in Welfare*. Philadelphia: Temple University Press.

Brooks-Gunn, Jeanne, Greg J. Duncan, Pam Kato, and Naomi Sealand. 1992. "Do Neighborhoods Influence Child and Adolescent Behavior?" Paper presented at the Conference on the Urban Underclass, University of Michigan, Ann Arbor, Mich., June.

Burtless, Gary. 1987. "The Work Response to a Guaranteed Income: A Survey of Experimental Evidence." In Alicia Munnell, ed., *Lessons from the Income Maintenance Experiments*. Boston: Federal Reserve Bank.

Cain, Glen G. 1987. "Negative Income Tax Experiments and the Issues of Marital Stability and Family Composition." In Alicia Munnell, ed.,

Lessons from the Income Maintenance Experiments. Boston: Federal Reserve Bank.

Chambre, Susan M. 1985. "Role Orientation and Intergenerational Welfare Use." *Social Casework*, 25: 25–56.

Cherlin, Andrew J. 1981. *Marriage, Divorce, Remarriage.* Cambridge, Mass.: Harvard University Press.

Connell, James Patrick, Elizabeth Clifford, and Warren Crichlow. 1992. "Why Do Urban Students Leave School? Neighborhood, Family, and Motivational Influences." Paper presented at the Conference on the Urban Underclass, University of Michigan, Ann Arbor, Mich., June.

Corcoran, Mary, Greg Duncan, Gerald Gurin, and Patricia Gurin. 1985. "Myth and Reality: The Causes and Persistence of Poverty." *Journal of Policy Analysis and Management*, 4: 516–536.

Corcoran, Mary, Roger Gordon, Deborah Laren, and Gary Solon. 1987. "Intergenerational Transmission of Education, Income, and Earnings." University of Michigan, Ann Arbor, Mich., July. Mimeo.

Crane, Jonathon. 1991. "The Epidemic Theory of Ghettos and Neighborhood Effects on Dropping Out and Teenage Childbearing." *American Journal of Sociology*, 96: 1226–1259.

Danziger, Sheldon, George Jakubson, Saul Schwartz, and Eugene Smolensky. 1982. "Work and Welfare as Determinants of Female Poverty and Household Headship." *Quarterly Journal of Economics*, 98: 519–534.

Datcher, Linda. 1982. "Effects of Community and Family Background on Achievement." *Review of Economics and Statistics*, 64: 32–41.

Derthick, Martha. 1970. *The Influence of Federal Grants: Public Assistance in Massachusetts.* Cambridge, Mass.: Harvard University Press.

———— 1975. *Uncontrollable Spending for Social Services Grants.* Washington, D.C.: Brookings Institution.

Duncan, Greg, and James Morgan. 1981. "Sense of Efficacy and Subsequent Change in Earnings—A Replication." *Journal of Human Resources*, 16: 649–657.

Ellwood, David T. 1986a. "Targeting the 'Would-Be' Long-Term Recipient: Who Should Be Served." Mathematica Policy Research, Princeton, N.J.

———— 1986b. "Working Off Welfare: Policies and Prospects for Self-Support." Institute for Research on Poverty, Madison, Wis.

———— 1988. *Poor Support.* New York: Basic Books.

Ellwood, David T., and E. Kathleen Adams. 1990. "Medicaid Mysteries:

Transitional Benefits, Medicaid Coverage, and Welfare Exits." *Health Care Financing Review*, 11: 119–131.

Ellwood, David T., and Mary Jo Bane. 1985. "The Impact of AFDC on Family Structure and Living Arrangements." In Ron G. Ehrenberg, ed., *Research in Labor Economics*, vol. 7. Greenwich, Conn.: JAI Press.

Ellwood, David T., and Jonathon Crane. 1990. "Family Change among Black Americans: What Do We Know?" *Journal of Economic Perspectives*, 4: 65–84.

Ellwood, David T., and David T. Rodda. 1991. "The Hazards of Work and Marriage: The Influence of Male Employment on Marriage Rates." Working paper no. H-90-5, Malcolm Wiener Center for Social Policy, John F. Kennedy School of Government, Harvard University, Cambridge, Mass.

Friedlander, Daniel, et al. 1985. *Maryland: Demonstration of State Work/Welfare Initiatives, Final Report on the Employment Initiatives Evaluation*. New York: Manpower Demonstration Research Corporation.

Friedlander, Daniel, and Judith M. Gueron. 1990. *Are High-Cost Services More Effective Than Low-Cost Services? Evidence from Experimental Evaluations of Welfare-to-Work Programs*. New York: Manpower Demonstration Research Corporation.

Gardiner, John A., and Theodore Lyman. 1984. *The Fraud Control Game: State Responses to Fraud and Abuse in the AFDC and Medicaid Programs*. Bloomington, Ind.: Indiana University Press.

Garfinkel, Irwin, and Sara McLanahan. 1986. *Single Mothers and Their Children*. Washington, D.C.: Urban Institute.

Goodban, Nancy. 1985. "Psychological Impact of Being on Welfare." *Social Service Review*, 59: 403–422.

Goodwin, Leonard. 1972. *Do the Poor Want to Work?* New York: Vintage Books.

——— 1983. *Causes and Cures for Welfare*. Lexington, Mass.: Lexington Books.

Gritz, R. Mark, and Thomas McCurdy. 1991. "Patterns of Welfare Utilization and Multiple Program Participation among Young Women." Stanford University, Stanford, Calif.

Groeneveld, Lyle P., Michael T. Hannan, and Nancy Tuma. 1983. "Marital Stability." *Final Report of the Seattle/Denver Income Maintenance Experiment*. Vol. 1: *Design and Results*. Washington, D.C.: U.S. Government Printing Office.

Grossman, Jean B., Rebecca Maynard, and Judith Roberts. 1985. "Reanalysis of the Effects of Selected Employment and Training Programs for Welfare Recipients." Report prepared for the U.S. Department of Health and Human Services. Mathematica Policy Research, Princeton, N.J.

Gueron, Judith M. 1986. *Work Initiatives for Welfare Recipients.* New York: Manpower Demonstration Research Corporation.

Gurin, Gerald, and Patricia Gurin. 1970. "Expectancy Theory in the Study of Poverty," *Journal of Social Policy,* 26: 83–104.

Hamilton, Gordon. 1962. "Separating Money and Services." *Social Work* 7: 2,128.

Hamilton, William L., Nancy Burstein, Elizabeth Davis, and Margaret Hargreaves. 1992. *New York Child Assistance Program: Interim Report on Program Impact.* Cambridge, Mass.: Abt Associates, June.

Handler, Joel. 1972. *Reforming the Poor: Welfare Policy, Federalism, and Morality.* New York: Basic Books.

Handler, Joel, and Ellen Jane Hollingsworth. 1971. *The "Deserving Poor": A Study of Welfare Administration.* Chicago: Markham Publishing.

Harrington, Michael. 1962. *The Other America.* New York: Macmillan.

Harris, Kathleen Mullan. 1992. "Work and Welfare among Single Mothers in Poverty." Paper presented at the APPAM Annual Research Conference, Denver, Colo., October.

Hayes, Cheryl D., ed. 1987. *Risking the Future: Adolescent Sexuality, Pregnancy, and Childbearing.* National Research Council, Panel on Adolescent Pregnancy and Childbearing. Washington, D.C.: National Academy Press.

Heckman, James, and Burton Singer. 1982. "Population Heterogeneity in Demographic Models." In Kenneth Land and Andrei Rogers, eds., *Multidimensional Mathematical Demography.* New York: Academic Press.

——— 1984. "A Method for Minimizing the Impact of Distributional Assumptions in Econometric Models for Duration Data." *Econometrica,* 52: 271–320.

Herr, Toby, Robert Halpern, and Aimee Conrad. 1991. "Changing What Counts: Re-thinking the Journey out of Welfare." Research and Policy Reports, Northwestern University Center for Urban Affairs and Policy Research, Evanston, Ill.

Hill, Martha, Sue Augustyniak, Greg Duncan, Gerald Gurin, Patricia Gurin, Jeffrey Liker, James Morgan, and Michael Ponza. 1985. *Motivation and Economic Mobility of the Poor.* Ann Arbor, Mich.: Institute for Social Research.

Hill, Martha, and Michael Ponza. 1986. "Does Welfare Dependency Beget Dependency?" Institute for Social Research, Ann Arbor, Mich. Mimeo.

Hoffman, Saul. 1987. "Dependency and Welfare Receipt: An Empirical Review." Hudson Institute, Indianapolis, Ind. Mimeo.

Hoffman, Saul, and Greg Duncan. 1986. "A Choice-Based Analysis of Remarriage and Welfare Decisions of Divorced Women." Institute for Social Research, Ann Arbor, Mich., August. Mimeo.

Hoshino, George. 1971. "The Public Welfare Worker: Advocate or Adversary?" *Public Welfare*, 29: 35–41.

Jargowsky, Paul A. Forthcoming. "Ghetto Poverty among Blacks in the 1980s." *Journal of Policy Analysis and Management.*

Jencks, Christopher, and Kathryn Edin. 1990. "The Real Welfare Problem." *American Prospect*, 1: 30–50.

Jencks, Christopher, and Susan E. Mayer. 1990. "The Social Consequences of Growing Up in a Poor Neighborhood." Chapter 4 in Laurence E. Lynn, Jr., and Michael G. H. McGeary, eds., *Inner-City Poverty in the United States.* Washington, D.C.: National Academy Press.

Kalbfleisch, John, and Ross Prentice. 1980. *The Statistical Analysis of Failure Time Data.* New York: John Wiley.

Kane, Thomas J. 1990. "The Caseworker-Client Relationship and Welfare Reform." Working paper no. H-90–9, Malcolm Wiener Center for Social Policy, John F. Kennedy School of Government, Harvard University, Cambridge, Mass.

Kaplan, H. Roy, and Curt Tausky. 1972. "Work and the Welfare Cadillac: The Functions of and Commitment to Work among the Hard Core Unemployed." *Social Problems*, 19: 469–484.

Katz, Lawrence, and Anne Case. 1991. "The Company You Keep: The Effects of Family and Neighborhood on Disadvantaged Youths." Working Paper no. 3705, National Bureau of Economic Research, Cambridge, Mass.

Katz, Michael. 1983. *Poverty and Policy in American History.* New York: Academic Press.

——— 1986. *In the Shadow of the Poorhouse.* New York: Basic Books.

Kaus, Mickey. 1986. "The Work Ethic State." *New Republic*, July 7, pp. 22–33.

Kessler, Ron C., and James McRae, Jr. 1982. "The Effects of Wives' Employment on the Mental Health of Married Men and Women." *American Sociological Review*, 47: 216–227.

King v. Smith. 1968. 392 U.S. 309.

Lancaster, Tony. 1979. "Econometric Methods for the Duration of Unemployment." *Econometrica*, 47: 939–956.

Leiby, James. 1978. *A History of Social Welfare and Social Work in the United States.* New York: Columbia University Press.

Lein, Laura. 1989. "Child-Serving Insitutions: A View from within the Community." Paper presented at the meetings of the Association for the Practice of Anthropology, April.

———— 1991. "The Formation of Community in Public Housing." Paper presented at the second annual Conference on Ethnic Minorities and Gender, University of Texas at Arlington, February.

Lerman, Robert. 1986. "Welfare Dependency: Facts and Correlates." Report prepared for the U.S. Department of Health and Human Services. Brandeis University, Waltham, Mass.

———— 1987. "Child Support and Dependency." Report prepared for the U.S. Department of Health and Human Services. Brandeis University, Waltham, Mass.

Levy, Frank. 1979. "The Labor Supply of Female Household Heads, or AFDC Work Incentives Don't Work Too Well." *Journal of Human Resources*, 14: 76–97.

Mare, Richard, and Christopher Winship. 1991. "Socioeconomic Change and the Decline of Marriage for Blacks and Whites." In Christopher Jencks and Paul E. Peterson, eds., *The Urban Underclass.* Washington, D.C.: Brookings Institution.

McFadden, Daniel. 1973. "Conditional Logit Analysis of Qualitative Choice Behavior." In P. Zarembka, ed., *Frontiers in Econometrics.* New York: Academic Press.

———— 1976. "Quantal Choice Analysis: A Survey." *Annals of Economic and Social Measurement*, 5: 363–390.

McLanahan, Sara. 1986. "Family Structure and Dependency: Early Transitions to Female Headship." Discussion paper no. 807, Institute for Research on Poverty, Madison, Wis.

Mead, Lawrence M. 1986. *Beyond Entitlement: The Social Obligations of Citizenship.* New York: Free Press.

Michel, Richard. 1980. "Participation Rates in the Aid to Families with Dependent Children Program, Part I." Working paper no. 1387–02, Urban Institute, Washington, D.C.

Moffitt, Robert. 1985. "A Problem with the Negative Income Tax." *Economic Letters*, 17: 261–265.

———— 1986. "Trends in AFDC Participation over Time: Evidence on Structural Change." Special report no. 41, Institute for Research on Poverty, Madison, Wis.

———— 1992. "Incentive Effects of the U.S. Welfare System: A Review." *Journal of Economic Literature*, 30: 1–61.

Moffitt, Robert, and Barbara Wolfe. 1989. "The Effects of Medicaid on Welfare Dependency and Work." Report prepared for the U.S. Department of Health and Human Services. National Bureau of Economic Research, Cambridge, Mass., June.

Murray, Charles. 1984. *Losing Ground: American Social Policy 1950–1980*. New York: Basic Books.

Murray, Charles, and Deborah Laren. 1986. "According to Age: Longitudinal Profiles of AFDC Recipients and the Poor by Age Group." Paper prepared for the Working Seminar on the Family and American Welfare Policy, September.

Nathan, Richard. 1993. *Turning Promises into Performance: The Management Challenge of Implementing Workfare*. New York: Columbia University Press.

National Commission on Children. 1991. *Beyond Rhetoric: A New American Agenda for Children and Families*. Washington, D.C.: U.S. Government Printing Office.

Nerlove, Mark, and S. J. Press. 1973. "Univariate and Multivariate Log-Linear and Logistic Models." Rand Corporation, Santa Monica, Calif.

New York State Department of Social Welfare. 1963. *Bulletin*, no. 159a, December 16.

Nightingale, Demetra Smith, Douglas A. Wissoker, Lynn C. Burbridge, D. Lee Bawden, and Neal Jeffries. 1991. *Evaluation of the Massachusetts Employment and Training (ET) Program*. Urban Institute Report no. 91–1. Washington, D.C.: Urban Institute Press.

N.Y. DSW. *See* New York State Department of Social Welfare.

O'Neill, June. 1990. *Work and Welfare in Massachusetts: An Evaluation of the ET Program*. Boston: Pioneer Institute for Public Policy Research.

O'Neill, June, Douglas Wolf, Laurie Bassi, and Michael Hannan. 1984. *An Analysis of Time on Welfare*. Report to the U.S. Department of Health and Human Services. Washington, D.C.: Urban Institute.

Parsons, Talcott, and Robert Bales, eds. 1955. *Family, Socialization, and Interaction Process*. Glencoe, Ill.: Free Press.

Pavetti, LaDonna. 1993. "The Dynamics of Welfare and Work: Exploring the Process by Which Women Work Their Way Off Welfare." Ph.D. dissertation, Harvard University.

Pechman, Joseph A., ed. 1992. *Fulfilling America's Promise: Social Policies for the 1990s.* Ithaca, N.Y.: Cornell University Press.

Peterson, Paul E., and Mark C. Rom, 1990. *Welfare Magnets: A New Case for a National Standard.* Washington, D.C.: Brookings Institution.

Piliavin, Irving, and Alan Gross. 1977. "The Effects of Separation of Services and Income Maintenance on AFDC Recipients." *Social Service Review*, 51: 389–406.

Piven, Frances Fox, and Richard Cloward. 1971. *Regulating the Poor.* New York: Vintage Books.

——— 1977. *Poor Peoples' Movements.* New York: Pantheon.

Plant, Mark. 1984. "An Empirical Analysis of Welfare Dependence," *American Economic Review*, 74: 673–682.

Polit, Denise, and Joseph O'Hara. 1989. "Support Services." Chapter 6 in Phoebe H. Cottingham and David T. Ellwood, eds., *Welfare Policy for the 1990s.* Cambridge, Mass.: Harvard University Press.

Preston, Sam H., and Alan T. Richards. 1975. "The Influence of Women's Work Opportunities on Marriage Rates." *Demography*, 12: 209–222.

Rainwater, Lee. 1987. "Class, Culture, Poverty, and Welfare." Report prepared for the U.S. Department of Health and Human Services. Harvard University, Cambridge, Mass.

Riccio, James, and Daniel Friedlander. 1992. *GAIN: Program Strategies, Participation Patterns, and First-Year Impacts in Six Counties.* New York: Manpower Demonstration Research Corporation.

Ricketts, Errol, and Isabel Sawhill. 1986. "Defining and Measuring the Underclass." Paper presented at the meetings of the American Economic Association, December.

Roper Organization. N.d. *The 1985 Virginia Slims American Women's Poll.*

Ross, Catherine, John Mirowsky, and John Huber. 1983. "Marriage Patterns and Depression." *American Sociological Review*, 48: 809–823.

Ross, Heather, and Isabel Sawhill. 1975. *Time of Transition: The Growth of Families Headed by Women.* Washington, D.C.: Urban Institute.

Shapiro v. Thompson. 1969. 394 U.S. 618.

Simon, William H. 1983. "Legality, Bureaucracy, and Class in the Welfare System." *Yale Law Journal*, 92: 1198–1269.

Social Security Administration. 1989. *Social Security Bulletin, Annual Statistical Supplement.*

Social Security Administration, Office of Payment and Eligibility Quality,

Division of AFDC Quality Control. 1980. "Aid to Families with Dependent Children, Official Case and Payment Error Rates for April–September 1973 through October–March 1979." May. Unpublished mimeo.

Sosin, Michael. 1986. "Legal Rights and Welfare Change, 1960–1980." In Sheldon Danziger and Daniel Weinberg, eds., *Fighting Poverty: What Works and What Doesn't*. Cambridge, Mass.: Harvard University Press.

Spalter-Roth, Heidi Hartmann, Linda Andrews, and Usha Sunkara. 1991. "Combining Work and Welfare: An Alternative Anti-Poverty Strategy." Report to the Ford Foundation.

SSA. *See* Social Security Administration.

SSA–OPEQ. *See* Social Security Administration, Office of Payment and Eligibility Quality.

Stack, Carol. 1974. *All Our Kin*. New York: Harper & Row.

Steiner, Gilbert. 1966. *Social Insecurity: The Politics of Welfare*. Chicago: Rand McNally.

Survey Research Center. 1984. *User Guide for the Panel Study of Income Dynamics*. Ann Arbor, Mich.: Survey Research Center, University of Michigan.

Testa, Mark. 1990. "Joblessness and Absent Fatherhood in the Inner City." School of Social Services Administration, University of Chicago, Chicago, Ill.

Urban Systems Research and Engineering, Inc. 1982. "Transitions from Welfare to Work: Evaluation Design." Prepared for the Assistant Secretary for Planning and Evaluation, U.S. Department of Health and Human Services, Washington, D.C.

U.S. Bureau of the Census. 1984. *1980 Census of the Population. Detailed Population Characteristics: U.S. Summary*. Washington, D.C.: U.S. Government Printing Office.

——— 1985a. *Money Income and Poverty Status of Families and Persons in the United States: 1984 (Advance Data from the March 1985 Current Population Survey)*. Current Population Reports, series P-60, no. 149. Washington, D.C.: U.S. Government Printing Office.

——— 1985b. *1980 Census of Population*, Vol. 2: *Subject Reports: Poverty Areas in Large Cities*. PC80–2–8D. Washington, D.C.: U.S. Government Printing Office.

——— 1985c. *Statistical Abstract of the United States: 1986*. 106th ed. Washington, D.C.: U.S. Government Printing Office.

——— 1987. *Who's Minding the Kids? Child Care Arrangements: Winter*

1984–1985. Current Population Reports, series P-70, no. 9. Washington, D.C.: U.S. Government Printing Office.

———— 1991. *Poverty in the United States: 1990,* Current Population Reports, series P-60, no. 175. Washington, D.C.: U.S. Government Printing Office.

———— 1992. *Poverty in the United States: 1991,* Current Population Reports, series P-60, no. 181. Washington, D.C.: U.S. Government Printing Office.

U.S. Census. *See* U.S. Bureau of the Census.

U.S. Congress. 1988. *Family Support Act of 1988,* October 13, 1988, 100th Congress, 2d sess., Public Law 100-485.

U.S. Department of Housing and Urban Development. 1991. "Schedule B. Fair Market Rents for Existing Housing." *Federal Register,* 156 (187): 49024. September 26.

U.S. House. *See* U.S. House of Representatives.

U.S. House, Ways and Means. *See* U.S. House of Representatives, Committee on Ways and Means.

U.S. House of Representatives. Committee on Ways and Means. 1987. *Background Material and Data on Programs within the Jurisdiction of the Committee on Ways and Means.* Washington, D.C.: U.S. Government Printing Office, 1987.

———— 1990. *1990 Green Book: Background Material and Data on Programs within the Jurisdiction of the Committee on Ways and Means.* Washington, D.C.: U.S. Government Printing Office.

———— 1991. *1991 Green Book: Background Material and Data on Programs within the Jurisdiction of the Committee on Ways and Means.* Washington, D.C.: U.S. Government Printing Office.

———— 1992. *1992 Green Book: Background Material and Data on Programs within the Jurisdiction of the Committee on Ways and Means.* Washington, D.C.: U.S. Government Printing Office.

———— 1993. *1993 Green Book: Background Material and Data on Programs within the Jurisdiction of the Committee on Ways and Means.* Washington, D.C.: U.S. Government Printing Office.

U.S. HUD. *See* U.S. Department of Housing and Urban Development.

Weeks, Gregory C. 1991. "Leaving Public Assistance in Washington State." Washington State Institute for Public Policy, Evergreen State College, Olympia, Wash.

Wilson, William J. 1985. "Cycles of Deprivation and the Underclass Debate." *Social Service Review.*

———— 1987. *The Truly Disadvantaged.* Chicago: University of Chicago Press.

Wilson, William J., and Katherine M. Neckerman. 1986. "Poverty and Family Structure: The Widening Gap between Evidence and Public Policy Issues." In Sheldon Danziger and Daniel Weinberg, eds., *Fighting Poverty: What Works and What Doesn't.* Cambridge, Mass.: Harvard University Press.

Winkler, Anne. 1991. "The Incentive Effects of Medicaid on Women's Labor Supply." *Journal of Human Resources,* 26: 308–327.

Working Seminar on the Family and American Welfare Policy. 1987. *The New Consensus on Family and Welfare.* Washington, D.C.: American Enterprise Institute.

Zelnick, Melvin, John Kanter, and Kathleen Ford. 1981. *Sex and Pregnancy in Adolescents.* Beverly Hills, Calif.: Sage Publications.

Index